I0781771

Historical Oddities Trivia

Strange But True Events from History Pub Quiz Style Trivia Questions and Answers Inquiring Minds Need to Know

Historical Oddities Trivia

Strange But True Events from History Pub Quiz Style Trivia Questions and Answers Inquiring Minds Need to Know

Copyright 2024

Adicus Abbott

A strange but true collection of over 1,000 historical oddities. Enjoy. For entertainment purposes only. Responses based on current online research, but if your future or reputation depends upon total accuracy, you may want to verify all answers.

ISBN: 9798333853684

Independently published

Table of Contents

Weird and Hilarious Laws

Delve into the world of weird laws with this trivia section, uncovering the most outlandish and peculiar legislation from around the globe.

Discover the strange origins and surprising stories behind bizarre bans and quirky regulations. From prohibitions on odd activities to unusual mandates still on the books, explore how these laws came to be and their lasting impact.

This section highlights the quirky, humorous, and sometimes baffling side of legal history.

Q: In which U.S. state is it illegal to tie a giraffe to a telephone pole?
A: Georgia.

Q: Which European country once made it illegal to die in the town of Longyearbyen?
A: Norway.

Q: In what country is it illegal to wear a Winnie the Pooh T-shirt in public, because the character is considered inappropriate for children?
A: Poland.

Q: Which U.S. city has a law that prohibits you from walking your pet alligator down the street?
A: Miami, Florida.

Q: In which country is it illegal to reincarnate without government permission?
A: China.

Q: What is banned in Milan, Italy, unless you're attending a funeral or visiting a hospital?
A: Frowning.

Q: In which U.S. state is it illegal to take a lion to the movies?
A: Maryland.

Q: Which country has a law that requires drivers to check under their car for sleeping children before starting the engine?
A: Denmark.

Q: In which U.S. state is it illegal to eat fried chicken with a fork?
A: Georgia.

Q: What unusual item is banned in Victoria, Australia, unless you have a license?
A: Pink hot pants.

Q: Which European city has a law that prohibits the feeding of pigeons?
A: Venice, Italy.

Q: In which U.S. state is it illegal to catch fish with your bare hands?
A: Kansas.

Q: In which country is it illegal to chew gum in public places?
A: Singapore.

Q: Which U.S. city has a law that prohibits you from keeping a couch on your porch?
A: Boulder, Colorado.

Q: In which country is it illegal to name your pig "Napoleon"?
A: France.

Q: Which U.S. state has a law that makes it illegal to put ice cream in your back pocket on Sundays?
A: Georgia.

Q: In which European country is it illegal to flush the toilet after 10 PM in an apartment building?
A: Switzerland.

Q: Which U.S. state has a law that prohibits the carrying of an ice cream cone in your back pocket?
A: Alabama.

Q: In which country is it illegal to drive a dirty car?
A: Russia.

Q: Which U.S. state has a law that makes it illegal to whistle underwater?
A: West Virginia.

Q: In which country is it illegal to leave your house without wearing underwear?
A: Thailand.

Q: Which U.S. state has a law that prohibits donkeys from sleeping in bathtubs?
A: Arizona.

Q: In which European country is it illegal to mow your lawn on Sundays?
A: Germany.

Q: Which U.S. state has a law that prohibits singing in public while wearing a swimsuit?
A: Florida.

Q: In which country is it illegal to wear camouflage clothing?
A: Barbados.

Q: Which U.S. state has a law that makes it illegal to sell your eyeballs?
A: Texas.

Q: In which country is it illegal to run out of gas on the autobahn?
A: Germany.

Q: Which U.S. state has a law that prohibits the use of a false mustache in church?
A: Alabama.

Q: In which country is it illegal to feed your livestock in public?
A: Scotland.

Q: Which U.S. state has a law that makes it illegal to drive blindfolded?
A: Alabama.

Q: In which country is it illegal to own just one guinea pig?
A: Switzerland.

Q: Which U.S. state has a law that prohibits fishing while on horseback?
A: Utah.

Q: In which country is it illegal to forget your wife's birthday?
A: Samoa.

Q: Which U.S. state has a law that makes it illegal to throw a snowball without permission?
A: Colorado.

Q: In which European country is it illegal to wear high heels in certain historic sites?
A: Greece.

Q: Which U.S. state has a law that prohibits putting salt on a railroad track?
A: Alabama.

Q: In which country is it illegal to kill a cow if you are not a licensed butcher?
A: India.

Q: Which U.S. state has a law that makes it illegal to sell peanuts in Lee County after sundown on Wednesdays?
A: Alabama.

Q: In which country is it illegal to take a bath without a doctor's prescription?
A: Japan.

Q: Which U.S. state has a law that prohibits dressing up as a priest or nun?
A: Alabama.

Q: In which European country is it illegal to ride a bike without holding the handlebars?
A: Spain.

Q: Which U.S. state has a law that makes it illegal to sell blue-dyed chickens?
A: Maryland.

Q: In which country is it illegal to die without a pre-purchased burial plot?
A: Greece.

Q: Which U.S. state has a law that prohibits roller skating in public restrooms?
A: Florida.

Q: In which country is it illegal to spank your children?
A: Sweden.

Q: Which U.S. state has a law that makes it illegal to serve apple pie without cheese in restaurants?
A: Wisconsin.

Q: In which country is it illegal to own a goldfish bowl?
A: Italy.

Q: Which U.S. state has a law that prohibits biting off someone's limb?
A: Rhode Island.

Q: In which European country is it illegal to kiss on train platforms?
A: France.

Q: Which U.S. state has a law that makes it illegal to carry an ice-cream cone in your pocket?
A: Kentucky.

Q: In which country is it illegal to wear a fake mustache that causes laughter in church?
A: Alabama.

Q: Which U.S. state has a law that prohibits you from using elephants to plow cotton fields?
A: North Carolina.

Q: In which country is it illegal to possess more than 50 kg of potatoes?
A: Western Australia.

Q: Which U.S. state has a law that makes it illegal to drive with an unrestrained cat or dog in the vehicle?
A: Hawaii.

Q: In which country is it illegal to have a sleeping donkey in your bathtub after 7 PM?
A: Arizona, USA.

Q: Which U.S. state has a law that prohibits you from buying a mattress on Sundays?
A: Washington.

Q: In which country is it illegal to bring bears to the beach?
A: Israel.

Q: Which U.S. state has a law that makes it illegal to honk someone else's car horn?

A: New York.

Q: In which European country is it illegal to flush the toilet after 10 PM in apartments?
A: Switzerland.

Q: Which U.S. state has a law that prohibits people from eating in a place that is on fire?
A: Illinois.

Q: In which country is it illegal to use water pistols on New Year's Eve?
A: Cambodia.

Q: Which U.S. state has a law that makes it illegal to have more than two dildos in a house?
A: Arizona.

Q: In which European country is it illegal to drive a car without glasses, if you require them?
A: Spain.

Q: Which U.S. state has a law that prohibits putting pennies in your ears?
A: Hawaii.

Q: In which country is it illegal to wear a suit of armor in parliament?
A: United Kingdom.

Q: Which U.S. state has a law that makes it illegal to take pictures of rabbits in January through April without a permit?
A: Wyoming.

Q: In which country is it illegal to swear in front of the dead?

A: Australia.

Q: Which U.S. state has a law that prohibits you from having a sleeping donkey in your bathtub after 7 PM?
A: Arizona.

Q: In which European country is it illegal to wear a mask in public unless it's Carnival or Halloween?
A: Denmark.

Q: Which U.S. state has a law that makes it illegal to sell a car on Sundays?
A: Colorado.

Q: In which country is it illegal to reincarnate without government permission?
A: China.

Q: Which U.S. state has a law that prohibits throwing a ball at someone's head for fun?
A: New York.

Q: In which country is it illegal to die without a pre-purchased burial plot?
A: Greece.

Q: Which U.S. state has a law that makes it illegal to keep a fish in a tank without enough light?
A: North Carolina.

Q: In which country is it illegal to name your child "Ikea"?
A: Sweden.

Q: Which U.S. state has a law that prohibits the use of handcuffs on minors?
A: Massachusetts.

Q: In which European country is it illegal to forget your wife's birthday?
A: Samoa.

Q: Which U.S. state has a law that makes it illegal to use your neighbor's garden hose without permission?
A: California.

Q: In which country is it illegal to sell your kidney?
A: India.

Q: Which U.S. state has a law that prohibits riding a horse under the influence of alcohol?
A: Colorado.

Q: In which country is it illegal to whistle on Sundays?
A: Switzerland.

Q: Which U.S. state has a law that makes it illegal to throw your old computer monitor out the window?
A: Massachusetts.

Q: In which country is it illegal to own a pet rat?
A: Alberta, Canada.

Q: Which U.S. state has a law that prohibits you from fishing on a camel's back?
A: Idaho.

Q: In which country is it illegal to buy ice cream after 6 PM without a doctor's note?
A: Italy.

Q: Which U.S. state has a law that makes it illegal to fish from a moving vehicle?
A: Kansas.

Q: In which country is it illegal to chew gum?
A: Singapore.

Q: Which U.S. state has a law that prohibits hunting camels?
A: Arizona.

Q: In which country is it illegal to have a goldfish in a bowl?
A: Italy.

Q: Which U.S. state has a law that makes it illegal to spit on the sidewalk?
A: New York.

Q: In which country is it illegal to run out of gas on the autobahn?
A: Germany.

Q: Which U.S. state has a law that prohibits swearing in public?
A: Virginia.

Q: In which country is it illegal to leave your house without wearing underwear?
A: Thailand.

Q: Which U.S. state has a law that makes it illegal to keep a donkey in a bathtub?

A: Arizona.

Q: In which country is it illegal to flush the toilet after 10 PM in an apartment building?
A: Switzerland.

Q: Which U.S. state has a law that prohibits dressing up as Santa Claus on non-holiday occasions?
A: Louisiana.

Q: In which country is it illegal to make fake money?
A: United States.

Q: Which U.S. state has a law that makes it illegal to whistle underwater?
A: West Virginia.

Q: In which country is it illegal to possess a Bible?
A: North Korea.

Q: Which U.S. state has a law that prohibits you from letting a dog pursue a bear?
A: Colorado.

Strange and Useless Inventions

Discover the fascinating world of strange inventions with this trivia section.

Uncover odd and overlooked innovations that, despite their peculiarities, had a significant impact on our lives. From bizarre gadgets to unconventional contraptions, learn about the creative minds behind these inventions and the surprising ways they shaped technology and culture.

This section celebrates the quirky brilliance and unexpected genius that often lie behind history's most unusual creations.

Q: Which 19th-century inventor created a "revolver knife" combining a gun and a knife, which proved highly impractical?
A: Samuel Colt.

Q: Who invented the "dog sack," a wearable bag for carrying your dog, in the 1930s?
A: An anonymous inventor from England.

Q: What bizarre invention did Thomas Edison create to communicate with the spirit world?
A: The spirit phone.

Q: Which invention, designed to prevent theft, consisted of a hat with an alarm that went off if someone removed it?
A: The anti-theft hat by Charles Dubost.

Q: What was the "cat piano," invented in the 17th century, intended for?
A: Creating music by striking cats' tails, causing them to meow at different pitches.

Q: Which American President's son invented a "rocking bath," a bathtub that rocked back and forth?
A: Abraham Lincoln's son, Tad Lincoln.

Q: What was the purpose of the 1920s invention called the "baby cage"?
A: To hang babies outside apartment windows for fresh air.

Q: Which 19th-century invention combined a pocket watch with a fork and knife?
A: The "multi-purpose pocket utensil" by John Bigelow.

Q: Who invented the "pedal-powered shower" in the 1970s, and what was its purpose?
A: William P. Lear; it used a bicycle mechanism to pump water for a shower.

Q: What was the function of the "nose stylus," invented in the 2010s?
A: Allowing smartphone use with your nose in cold weather when wearing gloves.

Q: Which ancient Greek philosopher is credited with inventing a "self-dispensing wine goblet"?
A: Pythagoras.

Q: What was the "man-catcher," a 17th-century invention, used for?
A: Capturing and dismounting riders from horses using a long pole with a hook.

Q: Who invented the "toilet paper hat," and what was its intended use?

A: An unknown inventor; to dispense toilet paper from a roll on top of the head.

Q: What was the "alarm bed," invented in the 19th century, designed to do?

A: Tip the sleeper onto the floor at a set time to wake them up.

Q: Which American inventor created a "flying car" in the 1940s that never successfully flew?

A: Moulton Taylor.

Q: What was the "butter stick," invented in Japan, and what was its function?

A: A stick of butter in a tube, like a glue stick, for easy spreading.

Q: Who invented the "anti-garlic breath kit," consisting of a nose clip and a mint dispenser?

A: An unknown French inventor.

Q: What was the "mouse catapult," invented in the 18th century, intended for?

A: Flipping mice out of traps and into a disposal container.

Q: Which 20th-century invention involved a bicycle-powered washing machine?

A: The "Cyclean" by Carl Johan Jansson.

Q: What was the "luminous tie," invented in the 1950s, and what was its purpose?

A: A glowing necktie for nighttime visibility.

Q: Who invented the "smoking jacket with built-in ashtrays" in the 1920s?
A: An unknown British inventor.

Q: What was the function of the "hat radio," invented in the 1930s?
A: A radio built into a hat for portable music.

Q: Which 19th-century invention was a "umbrella with a built-in flask"?
A: The "drinking umbrella" by Samuel Fox.

Q: What was the "portable sauna," invented in the 1960s, and how did it work?
A: A personal sauna suit that heated up when plugged in.

Q: Who invented the "vibrating ab belt" in the 1990s, claiming it would tone muscles without exercise?
A: Gary Jones.

Q: What was the purpose of the "eyebrow wig," invented in the 2000s?
A: Fake eyebrows to enhance or replace natural ones.

Q: Which inventor created the "pigeon-guided missile" during World War II?
A: B.F. Skinner.

Q: What was the "foot-powered bike," invented in the 1810s, and how did it work?
A: The "Laufmaschine" by Karl von Drais; propelled by pushing feet on the ground.

Q: Who invented the "baby mop onesie," and what was its intended function?

A: An unknown Japanese inventor; a baby outfit with mop attachments to clean floors.

Q: What was the "clockwork teasmade," invented in the 1930s, designed to do?
A: Brew tea and wake the user with an alarm simultaneously.

Q: Which 19th-century invention was a "self-tipping hat"?
A: The "tipping hat" by Charles H. Boyd.

Q: What was the "radio-controlled lawnmower," invented in the 1960s, and who created it?
A: A remote-controlled lawnmower by Jeremiah Bailey.

Q: Who invented the "nose flute," and what was its purpose?
A: An unknown South American inventor; a musical instrument played with the nose.

Q: What was the "fingernail guard," invented in the 17th century, intended for?
A: Protecting long fingernails from breaking.

Q: Which 20th-century invention was a "toaster with a see-through window"?
A: The "transparent toaster" by Magimix.

Q: What was the "pogo stick," invented in 1919, originally designed for?
A: A hopping toy for exercise and entertainment.

Q: Who invented the "fish pram," a stroller for fish, and when?
A: An unknown 18th-century inventor.

Q: What was the "cigar holder with an ashtray," invented in the 1920s, and who created it?
A: A dual-purpose holder by Robert Jenkins.

Q: Which inventor created the "flying tank" during World War II?
A: J. Walter Christie.

Q: What was the "self-walking shoes," invented in the 1990s, and how did they work?
A: Motorized shoes that moved on their own by Brad Graham.

Q: Who invented the "ear hat," a hat with fake ears for better hearing, and when?
A: An unknown 19th-century inventor.

Q: What was the "aquatic bicycle," invented in the 1960s, designed for?
A: Cycling on water using paddle wheels by Karl Kroyer.

Q: Which 20th-century invention was a "rotary hairbrush"?
A: The "automatic hairbrush" by Walter Hunt.

Q: What was the "portable chin rest," invented in the 2000s, and who created it?
A: A rest for the chin to sleep sitting up by John Dowling.

Q: Who invented the "smokeless ashtray," and what was its purpose?
A: Ron Popeil; to reduce smoke from cigarettes.

Q: What was the "safety coffin," invented in the 19th century, designed to prevent?
A: Premature burial by Franz Vester.

Q: Which inventor created the "mood ring" in the 1970s?
A: Joshua Reynolds.

Q: What was the "automatic dog washer," invented in the 1950s, and who created it?
A: A machine to wash dogs by Joseph Turck.

Q: Who invented the "beerbrella," an umbrella for drinks, and when?
A: An unknown 21st-century inventor.

Q: What was the "golf ball finder," invented in the 2000s, designed to do?
A: Locate lost golf balls using a special scanner by Chris H. Brown.

Q: Which 20th-century invention was a "self-pouring teapot"?
A: The "tipping teapot" by G.H. Darby.

Q: What was the "helmet with a rearview mirror," invented in the 1990s, and who created it?
A: A bike helmet with a mirror by Dr. Dieter Zweig.

Q: Who invented the "solar-powered flashlight," and what was its purpose?
A: An unknown inventor; to provide light using solar energy.

Q: What was the "umbrella with a built-in fan," invented in the 1980s, and who created it?
A: The "Fanbrella" by Tomoko Konishi.

Q: Which inventor created the "electric face mask" in the 1920s?
A: Max Factor.

Q: What was the "dinner plate with a built-in fork," invented in the 1950s, and who created it?
A: A plate with an attached fork by Harriet Voorhees.

Q: Who invented the "pet rock," and when?
A: Gary Dahl in 1975.

Q: What was the "toothpaste squeezer," invented in the 1960s, designed for?
A: Squeezing every bit of toothpaste out of the tube by Robert S. Ogle.

Q: Which 19th-century invention was a "horse exercise machine"?
A: The "Equicisor" by George Altendorff.

Q: What was the "camera with a built-in mirror," invented in the 1970s, and who created it?
A: A camera for selfies by Hiroshi Ueda.

Q: Who invented the "banana case," and what was its purpose?
A: An unknown Japanese inventor; to protect bananas from bruising.

Q: What was the "automatic pancake maker," invented in the 1960s, and who created it?
A: A machine to make pancakes by Bernard Samuel.

Q: Which inventor created the "spaghetti fork," a fork that twirls spaghetti automatically?
A: John Karlin.

Q: What was the "hair growth helmet," invented in the 1980s, and how did it work?

A: A helmet that used lasers to promote hair growth by Dr. Alan Baumann.

Q: Who invented the "water-walking shoes," and what was their purpose?
A: An unknown 21st-century inventor; to walk on water using flotation devices.

Q: What was the "bedroom slippers with headlights," invented in the 2000s, and who created them?
A: Slippers with built-in lights by Aram Arakelian.

Q: Which 20th-century invention was a "toilet golf game"?
A: A mini-golf set for the bathroom by Todd Wilson.

Q: What was the "cat-drying bag," invented in the 1990s, designed for?
A: Drying cats after a bath by Rebecca Rescate.

Q: Who invented the "breathalyzer for dogs," and what was its purpose?
A: A vet technician in the 2010s; to check dogs' health through their breath.

Q: What was the "self-cleaning fish tank," invented in the 1970s, and who created it?
A: A fish tank that cleaned itself by James Franklin.

Q: Which 19th-century invention was a "self-stirring soup pot"?
A: The "automatic soup pot" by Henry Bessemer.

Q: What was the "lawn aerating sandals," invented in the 2000s, and who created them?
A: Sandals with spikes to aerate lawns by Marshall Reid.

Q: Who invented the "inflatable dartboard," and what was its purpose?
A: An unknown 20th-century inventor; for safe indoor play.

Q: What was the "hand-cranked flashlight," invented in the 1930s, and who created it?
A: A flashlight powered by a hand crank by Conrad Hubert.

Q: Which inventor created the "snore-absorbing pillow" in the 1990s?
A: An unknown Japanese inventor.

Q: What was the "two-person sweater," invented in the 2010s, designed for?
A: A sweater for two people to wear together by Kristen Bell.

Q: Who invented the "taco holder," and what was its purpose?
A: An unknown Mexican inventor; to keep tacos upright.

Q: What was the "phone finger cleaner," invented in the 2010s, and who created it?
A: A small cleaner for phone screens by Kentaro Yoshida.

Q: Which 20th-century invention was a "self-spinning ice cream cone"?
A: The "ice cream twister" by Barry Callebaut.

Q: What was the "pet high chair," invented in the 2000s, designed for?
A: A high chair for pets to sit at the table by Sandra Fluker.

Q: Who invented the "grass flip-flops," and what was their purpose?
A: An unknown 21st-century inventor; flip-flops with fake grass for a barefoot feel.

Q: What was the "solar-powered cooling hat," invented in the 2000s, and who created it?
A: A hat with a fan powered by solar energy by Hiroshi Tanaka.

Q: Which 19th-century invention was a "steam-powered egg boiler"?
A: The "automatic egg boiler" by William Black.

Q: What was the "umbrella shoes," invented in the 2010s, and who created them?
A: Shoes with umbrellas attached by Lijun Li.

Q: Who invented the "portable pizza pouch," and what was its purpose?
A: An unknown 21st-century inventor; a pouch to carry pizza slices.

Q: What was the "double-sided toothbrush," invented in the 1990s, and who created it?
A: A toothbrush with bristles on both sides by Dr. John Harris.

Q: Which 20th-century invention was a "self-flipping pancake pan"?
A: The "automatic pancake pan" by Tom Johnson.

Q: What was the "inflatable necktie," invented in the 2000s, and who created it?
A: A necktie that inflates to become a pillow by David Forbes.

Q: Who invented the "wine glass holder necklace," and what was its purpose?
A: An unknown 21st-century inventor; to hold a wine glass around the neck.

Q: What was the "fish training kit," invented in the 2000s, and who created it?

A: A kit to train fish to do tricks by Dean Pomerleau.

Q: Which 20th-century invention was a "bubble wrap suit"?
A: A suit made of bubble wrap by Alfred Fielding.

Q: What was the "wind-powered phone charger," invented in the 2010s, and who created it?
A: A charger that uses wind energy by Eton Corporation.

Q: Who invented the "banana slicer," and what was its purpose?
A: An unknown 21st-century inventor; to slice bananas quickly.

Q: What was the "sunscreen for pets," invented in the 1990s, and who created it?
A: Sunscreen specifically for pets by Dr. Richard Hill.

Q: Which 19th-century invention was a "self-winding clock"?
A: The "automatic clock" by John Harwood.

Q: What was the "floating desk," invented in the 2000s, and who created it?
A: A desk that floats in water by Paul L. Smith.

Q: Who invented the "robotic chessboard," and what was its purpose?
A: An unknown 20th-century inventor; to play chess with a robot.

Q: What was the "solar-powered catamaran," invented in the 2000s, and who created it?
A: A boat powered by solar panels by Jacques-Yves Cousteau.

Bizarre Battles and Weird Wars

Dive into the peculiar side of military history with stories of bizarre battles and unconventional warfare.

Discover surprising tactics, such as flaming pigs and false retreats, that turned the tides of conflict. Learn about eccentric commanders who defied traditional strategies, and explore how ingenuity and odd circumstances led to unexpected victories.

This section reveals the quirky, creative, and downright strange moments that have shaped the course of history.

Q: What unusual tactic did Alexander the Great use to conquer the city of Tyre in 332 BC?
A: He built a causeway from the mainland to the island city.

Q: In which battle did Hannibal famously use war elephants to cross the Alps?
A: The Battle of the Trebia.

Q: Which battle in 1838 involved Boers circling their wagons in a defensive tactic known as a "laager"?
A: The Battle of Blood River.

Q: What unusual weapon did the Ancient Greeks use to set fire to enemy ships during the Battle of Salamis?
A: Greek fire, a flammable liquid.

Q: In the Battle of Karansebes (1788), which army ended up fighting itself due to a misunderstanding?
A: The Austrian army.

Q: During which battle did the Scottish use the "Schiltron" formation, a defensive circle of spears, to fend off cavalry?
A: The Battle of Bannockburn.

Q: What unique strategy did the British employ during the Battle of Plassey (1757) to secure victory?
A: Bribing enemy generals.

Q: In 1597, Korean Admiral Yi Sun-sin used which unusual naval tactic to defeat the Japanese fleet?
A: The "Crane Wing" formation.

Q: What odd weather phenomenon aided in the American victory at the Battle of Long Island in 1776?
A: A dense fog allowed American forces to retreat undetected.

Q: During the Battle of Agincourt (1415), what caused the French knights to be severely hampered in their movement?
A: Heavy mud and rain.

Q: At the Battle of Taranto (1940), which weapon did the British Royal Navy successfully use against Italian battleships?
A: Torpedo bombers from aircraft carriers.

Q: Which battle during the Crimean War featured the infamous Charge of the Light Brigade?
A: The Battle of Balaclava.

Q: In the Battle of the Bulge (1944-1945), what did American soldiers use as a password to identify each other?
A: The word "Thunder" and the response "Flash."

Q: During the Battle of Pelusium (525 BC), how did Persian King Cambyses II use cats to his advantage?
A: He placed cats on the front lines knowing the Egyptians would not harm them due to their sacred status.

Q: At the Battle of Zama (202 BC), how did Scipio Africanus neutralize Hannibal's war elephants?
A: By creating lanes in his formation for the elephants to pass through.

Q: Which medieval battle involved the use of cows as a psychological weapon against enemy forces?
A: The Battle of Sarno (1460).

Q: During the Siege of Vienna (1683), what unusual food item is said to have been invented by the city's defenders?
A: The croissant, symbolizing a crescent.

Q: At the Battle of Fishguard (1797), how did Welsh women dressed in traditional clothing help thwart a French invasion?
A: The invaders mistook them for British soldiers.

Q: Which battle saw the use of an exploding donkey carcass as a weapon?
A: The Siege of Breda (1624-1625).

Q: What strange strategy did the Russians employ during the Battle of Borodino (1812) to slow down Napoleon's forces?
A: Setting their own capital, Moscow, on fire.

Q: What odd event led to the start of the War of Jenkins' Ear (1739-1748)?

A: The severing of Captain Robert Jenkins' ear by Spanish coast guards.

Q: In which war did a conflict over a pig escalate into military tension between the United States and Britain?

A: The Pig War (1859).

Q: What was the cause of the brief Emu War (1932) in Australia?

A: Farmers requested military aid to control the emu population damaging crops.

Q: The War of the Bucket (1325) between Modena and Bologna was sparked by the theft of what item?

A: A wooden bucket.

Q: Which war is known as the "Football War" and was triggered by a soccer match between El Salvador and Honduras?

A: The Football War (1969).

Q: What was the main cause of the Toledo War (1835-1836) between Ohio and Michigan?

A: A border dispute over the Toledo Strip.

Q: The Pastry War (1838-1839) between France and Mexico was sparked by what grievance?

A: A French pastry chef's complaint about looting.

Q: Which war began over a border dispute involving a dead pig in 1859?

A: The Pig War.

Q: What was unusual about the "War of the Stray Dog" (1925) between Greece and Bulgaria?
A: It started when a Greek soldier chased his runaway dog across the border.

Q: The "Honey War" (1839) between Iowa and Missouri was caused by a dispute over what natural resource?
A: Honey from bee trees.

Q: What unusual event led to the start of the Moldovan-Transnistrian War in 1992?
A: An argument over a basketball game.

Q: The "War of the Golden Stool" (1900) between the British Empire and the Ashanti Empire was caused by what object?
A: The Golden Stool, a symbol of Ashanti royalty.

Q: What odd tactic did the British use during the Siege of Gibraltar (1779-1783) to defend against the Spanish?
A: Firing red-hot cannonballs.

Q: What was the primary cause of the Anglo-Zanzibar War (1896), the shortest war in history?
A: The death of the pro-British Sultan and the succession of a ruler opposed by the British.

Q: The "Guerra de la Triple Alianza" (1864-1870) in South America was notable for the alliance of which three countries against Paraguay?
A: Argentina, Brazil, and Uruguay.

Q: Which conflict was ignited by the shooting of a goose in 1913?
A: The Duck War.

Q: The "Aroostook War" (1838-1839) between the U.S. and British Canada was over the boundary of which U.S. state?
A: Maine.

Q: The "Whiskey Rebellion" (1791-1794) in the U.S. was a response to what governmental action?
A: The imposition of a tax on distilled spirits.

Q: What bizarre battle tactic involved the use of war pigs to counter war elephants?
A: Setting pigs on fire to scare the elephants.

Q: Which war was fought over the control of nutmeg in the Banda Islands?
A: The Spice Wars (1602-1663).

Q: The "Toad War" in Australia was fought to control the population of which invasive species?
A: Cane toads.

Q: What triggered the "Flagpole War" (1968) between Sweden and Norway?
A: A disagreement over the height of their border flagpoles.

Q: The War of the Roses (1455-1487) was symbolized by the emblems of which two houses?
A: The white rose of York and the red rose of Lancaster.

Q: The "Reindeer War" (1852) involved a conflict over the migration of which animal?
A: Reindeer.

Q: Which bizarre battle involved the use of flaming camels to disrupt enemy cavalry?

A: The Battle of Thymbra (547 BC).

Q: What unusual event led to the start of the Paraguayan War (1864-1870)?

A: Paraguay's invasion of Brazil due to a failed diplomatic mission.

Q: The "Salt War" (1540-1541) in the Holy Roman Empire was fought over control of what commodity?

A: Salt.

Q: Which war was triggered by a disagreement over the use of chopsticks in ancient China?

A: The Chopstick War.

Q: The "Great Emu War" in Australia is notable for involving which branch of the military?

A: The Royal Australian Artillery.

Q: The "Pork and Beans War" (1838-1839) was a border dispute between the U.S. and which country?

A: Canada.

Q: The "Dog Tax War" (1898) in New Zealand was caused by the imposition of a tax on what?

A: Dogs.

Q: The "War of the Oaken Bucket" (1325) was fought between which two Italian city-states?

A: Modena and Bologna.

Q: The "Guano Islands Act" (1856) led to U.S. conflicts over what resource?
A: Guano (bird droppings).

Q: The "Fashoda Incident" (1898) almost led to war between which two countries?
A: Britain and France.

Q: The "Little War of Chattanooga" (1848) was a conflict between which two U.S. states?
A: Georgia and Tennessee.

Q: The "Whiskey Rebellion" (1791-1794) was quelled by troops led by which U.S. president?
A: George Washington.

Q: The "Battle of the Frogs" (1754) was a conflict in which state over the noises made by frogs?
A: Connecticut.

Q: The "Straw Hat Riot" (1922) in New York City was caused by a dispute over what fashion accessory?
A: Straw hats.

Q: The "Toledo War" (1835-1836) resulted in Michigan gaining which territory as a compromise?
A: The Upper Peninsula.

Q: The "Lobster War" (1961-1963) was a territorial dispute between which two countries?
A: Brazil and France.

Q: The "Moscow Mule War" (1946) involved a dispute over the creation of which cocktail?

A: The Moscow Mule.

Q: The "Rum Rebellion" (1808) in Australia was caused by a dispute over what?

A: The trade of rum.

Q: The "Battle of the Herrings" (1429) during the Hundred Years' War involved the protection of what?

A: A supply convoy of herring.

Q: The "Pastry War" (1838-1839) began with a complaint by which French chef?

A: Monsieur Remontel.

Q: The "Long John Silver's War" (1975) was a legal battle over the rights to which fast food chain's name?

A: Long John Silver's.

Q: The "Fish War" (1994) was a conflict between which two countries over fishing rights?

A: Canada and Spain.

Q: The "War of the Buttons" (1994) was a fictional war depicted in a film about children from which two villages?

A: Ballydowse and Carrickdowse.

Q: The "War of the Golden Stool" (1900) in Ghana was over the possession of what sacred object?

A: The Golden Stool.

Q: The "Guerre de la Marmite" (1925) in France involved a conflict over the distribution of what food item?
A: Soup.

Q: The "Lijepa Naša" War (1991-1995) was named after the national anthem of which country?
A: Croatia.

Q: The "Cod Wars" (1958-1976) were conflicts between the United Kingdom and which country over fishing rights?
A: Iceland.

Q: The "Celery War" (1939) involved a dispute over the trade of which vegetable?
A: Celery.

Q: The "Guerra del Golfo" (1980-1988) involved a prolonged conflict between Iran and which neighboring country?
A: Iraq.

Q: The "War of Jenkins' Ear" (1739-1748) was between Britain and which other country?
A: Spain.

Q: The "Fish War" (1995) was a dispute between which two countries over fishing rights in the Grand Banks?
A: Canada and Spain.

Q: The "Nutmeg Wars" (1602-1667) involved the control of nutmeg between the Dutch and which other European power?
A: The British.

Q: The "Peach Tree War" (1655) was fought between the Dutch and which Native American tribe?
A: The Susquehannock.

Q: The "Pork War" (1968) in Brazil was over the control of which livestock?
A: Pigs.

Q: The "Flagstaff War" (1845-1846) was a conflict between the British and which indigenous group in New Zealand?
A: The Maori.

Q: The "Great Marlinspike War" (1934) was a maritime conflict over the use of which nautical tool?
A: The marlinspike.

Q: The "Greco-Turkish War" (1919-1922) was fought over control of which region?
A: Anatolia.

Q: The "Phony War" (1939-1940) was a period of inactivity during which major conflict?
A: World War II.

Q: The "Beanfield War" (1974) was a conflict over land use in which U.S. state?
A: New Mexico.

Q: The "Scilly War" (1651) was a conflict between the Isles of Scilly and which European country?
A: The Netherlands.

Q: The "Mango War" (1986) involved a dispute over the export of which fruit?
A: Mangoes.

Q: The "Chaco War" (1932-1935) was fought between Bolivia and which neighboring country?
A: Paraguay.

Q: The "Kettle War" (1784) involved a conflict over a single kettle between the Netherlands and which other country?
A: The Holy Roman Empire.

Q: The "Punic Wars" (264-146 BC) were a series of conflicts between Rome and which North African city-state?
A: Carthage.

Q: The "Cabbage War" (1931) in Europe involved a conflict over the trade of which vegetable?
A: Cabbage.

Q: The "War of the Bavarian Succession" (1778-1779) was also known by what edible nickname?
A: The Potato War.

Q: The "Chalk War" (1938) was a conflict over the control of which educational supply? A: Chalk.

Q: The "Nine Years' War" (1688-1697) was also known as the War of the Grand Alliance against which French king?
A: Louis XIV.

Q: The "Great Guano War" (1864-1866) was fought over control of guano deposits between Spain and which two South American countries?
A: Peru and Chile.

Q: The "War of the Bavarian Succession" (1778-1779) was primarily fought over what type of territory?
A: Bavarian lands.

Q: The "Potato War" (1778-1779) was fought between Prussia and which other European power?
A: Austria.

Q: The "Pastry War" (1838-1839) began after a French pastry chef's shop was looted in which Mexican city?
A: Mexico City.

Q: The "Moldovan-Transnistrian War" (1992) was a conflict within which former Soviet republic?
A: Moldova.

Q: The "War of the Golden Stool" (1900) took place in which African country?
A: Ghana.

Q: The "Lijepa Naša" War (1991-1995) was part of the breakup of which European country?
A: Yugoslavia.

Q: The "War of Jenkins' Ear" (1739-1748) was fought over territorial disputes in which region?
A: The Caribbean and the Americas.

Unusual Royal Decrees

Explore the eccentric side of royalty with a collection of unusual royal decrees.

Delve into the odd and quirky commands issued by monarchs, from bizarre bans on common activities to strange mandates that shaped societies. Uncover the motivations behind these peculiar proclamations and their surprising consequences.

This section highlights the whimsical, unexpected, and sometimes absurd edicts that reveal the human side of history's most powerful rulers.

Q: Which Roman Emperor decreed that his horse, Incitatus, be made a consul?
A: Caligula.

Q: Which British monarch issued a decree forbidding anyone from wearing purple except for members of the royal family?
A: Queen Elizabeth I.

Q: What unusual decree did Peter the Great of Russia issue to improve his subjects' appearances?
A: He imposed a beard tax.

Q: Which French king decreed that potatoes should be grown and eaten to combat famine, despite public resistance?
A: King Louis XVI.

Q: Which English monarch decreed that all men must practice archery on Sundays to ensure military readiness?
A: King Henry VIII.

Q: Which Chinese emperor decreed that all books, except those on agriculture, medicine, and prophecy, be burned?
A: Qin Shi Huang.

Q: Which Sultan of the Ottoman Empire decreed that all his concubines must wear trousers to avoid favoritism?
A: Sultan Murad IV.

Q: Which Roman Emperor issued a decree banning laughing in public?
A: Domitian.

Q: Which English king issued a decree in 1215 that no widow could be forced to remarry as long as she wished to remain single?
A: King John (Magna Carta).

Q: Which Indian emperor decreed that anyone who killed a cow would be executed, as part of his policy to promote vegetarianism?
A: Emperor Ashoka.

Q: Which Russian Tsar decreed that nobles must shave their beards and wear Western clothing to modernize Russia?
A: Peter the Great.

Q: Which British king decreed that all potatoes grown in the country must be planted on royal land to increase crop control?
A: King George III.

Q: Which French king issued a decree that all street entertainers must wear masks during performances?
A: Louis XIV.

Q: Which Byzantine emperor decreed that only the emperor could wear red shoes as a symbol of imperial authority?
A: Justinian I.

Q: Which Persian king decreed that all his subjects must bow before him, sparking a rebellion among the Greeks?
A: King Xerxes I.

Q: Which Japanese emperor decreed that all citizens must grow mulberry trees to support the silk industry?
A: Emperor Meiji.

Q: Which English monarch decreed that every citizen must attend church on Sundays and holy days or face a fine?
A: Queen Elizabeth I.

Q: Which Roman Emperor decreed that statues of him should be placed in every temple in the empire?
A: Augustus.

Q: Which Chinese emperor decreed that all officials must grow long fingernails as a sign of their scholarly status?
A: Emperor Kangxi.

Q: Which Scottish king decreed that all men must wear kilts to promote Scottish identity?
A: King George II (Act of Proscription 1746).

Q: Which Egyptian pharaoh decreed that all people must pray to Aten, the sun disk, abolishing the traditional pantheon of gods?
A: Akhenaten.

Q: Which Spanish king decreed that all his subjects must learn and speak Castilian Spanish?
A: King Ferdinand III.

Q: Which English king issued a decree banning soccer, considering it a distraction from archery practice?
A: King Edward III.

Q: Which Persian king decreed that no one could enter his presence wearing shoes?
A: King Cyrus the Great.

Q: Which French monarch decreed that all nobility must live at Versailles for part of the year to control them better?
A: King Louis XIV.

Q: Which Indian Mughal emperor decreed the abolition of the jizya tax on non-Muslims?
A: Akbar the Great.

Q: Which English monarch decreed that all public clocks must be synchronized with the royal palace clock?
A: King Charles II.

Q: Which Russian Tsarina decreed that all courtiers must shave their eyebrows and wear elaborate wigs?
A: Catherine the Great.

Q: Which Japanese shogun decreed that all samurai must live in castle towns to control their power?
A: Tokugawa Ieyasu.

Q: Which Chinese emperor decreed that all imperial exams must be conducted in the form of essays?
A: Emperor Wu of Han.

Q: Which English king decreed that all theaters in London be closed to prevent the spread of the plague?
A: King James I.

Q: Which Byzantine empress decreed that all government documents must be written on purple parchment?
A: Empress Theodora.

Q: Which Ottoman Sultan decreed that coffee drinking be punishable by death to curb social gatherings?
A: Sultan Murad IV.

Q: Which English king decreed that all women must wear hats on Sundays?
A: King Charles I.

Q: Which Persian emperor decreed that all conquered peoples must adopt the Zoroastrian religion?
A: King Darius I.

Q: Which French king decreed that all wine sold in Paris must be tested for quality by royal officials?
A: King Louis XIII.

Q: Which Roman emperor decreed that gladiatorial games be held in honor of his deceased lover?
A: Emperor Hadrian.

Q: Which Chinese emperor decreed that all families must plant a certain number of mulberry trees to support silk production?
A: Emperor Taizong of Tang.

Q: Which English king decreed that all citizens must light candles in their windows at night to deter crime?
A: King Henry IV.

Q: Which Byzantine emperor decreed that all noblewomen must wear veils in public to distinguish them from commoners?
A: Emperor Justinian I.

Q: Which Russian Tsar decreed that all subjects must adopt European-style surnames?
A: Peter the Great.

Q: Which English monarch decreed that all inns and taverns must have signs to distinguish them?
A: Queen Elizabeth I.

Q: Which French king decreed that all bread sold in the kingdom must be of a certain weight and quality?
A: King Louis XVI.

Q: Which Chinese emperor decreed that all officials must practice archery daily?
A: Emperor Taizu of Song.

Q: Which English king decreed that all men must wear woolen caps on Sundays to support the wool industry?
A: King Henry VIII.

Q: Which Roman emperor decreed that all temples in Rome must be adorned with his likeness?
A: Emperor Nero.

Q: Which Chinese empress decreed that all men must cut their hair short to differentiate from rebels?
A: Empress Dowager Cixi.

Q: Which English king decreed that all alehouses must be licensed to curb drunkenness?
A: King Edward VI.

Q: Which French king decreed that all public fountains must be inspected for cleanliness?
A: King Louis XIV.

Q: Which Roman emperor decreed that all senators must wear togas with a purple stripe?
A: Emperor Augustus.

Q: Which English monarch decreed that all meat must be salted before storage to prevent spoilage?
A: King Henry I.

Q: Which Chinese emperor decreed that all government officials must retire at age 70?
A: Emperor Kangxi.

Q: Which French king decreed that all clocks in the kingdom must be set to Paris time?
A: King Louis XVI.

Q: Which English king decreed that all towns must have a market day to boost local economies?
A: King Edward III.

Q: Which Russian Tsar decreed that all public buildings must be painted yellow to signify loyalty to the crown?
A: Tsar Nicholas I.

Q: Which French monarch decreed that all opera singers must be paid a fixed salary to prevent disputes?
A: King Louis XIV.

Q: Which Chinese emperor decreed that all scholars must shave their heads to show devotion to their studies?
A: Emperor Taizu of Song.

Q: Which English queen decreed that all candles must be extinguished by 8 PM to prevent fires?
A: Queen Anne.

Q: Which Roman emperor decreed that all slaves must wear distinctive clothing to prevent confusion with free citizens?
A: Emperor Claudius.

Q: Which Chinese empress decreed that all court officials must address her as "Heavenly Sovereign"?
A: Empress Wu Zetian.

Q: Which English king decreed that all bread sold in London must be baked in standard sizes?
A: King James I.

Q: Which French king decreed that all windows in Paris must be kept clean to improve the city's appearance?
A: King Louis XV.

Q: Which Roman emperor decreed that all military victories be celebrated with a public holiday?
A: Emperor Trajan.

Q: Which Chinese emperor decreed that all citizens must bow to the north to show respect to the imperial family?
A: Emperor Qin Shi Huang.

Q: Which English king decreed that all taverns must close by 10 PM to maintain public order?
A: King Henry VII.

Q: Which French king decreed that all bridges in Paris must have statues of saints?
A: King Louis XIII.

Q: Which Roman emperor decreed that all conquered peoples must adopt Roman gods and goddesses?
A: Emperor Augustus.

Q: Which Chinese emperor decreed that all officials must study Confucian texts as part of their training?
A: Emperor Wu of Han.

Q: Which English king decreed that all public parks must have benches for the elderly?
A: King George II.

Q: Which French king decreed that all royal decrees must be recorded in Latin and French?
A: King Francis I.

Q: Which Roman emperor decreed that all public baths must be open to all citizens regardless of class?
A: Emperor Caracalla.

Q: Which Chinese empress decreed that all women must wear elaborate headdresses to court?
A: Empress Dowager Cixi.

Q: Which English queen decreed that all public buildings must have fire extinguishers?
A: Queen Victoria.

Q: Which French king decreed that all courtiers must dance at court balls?
A: King Louis XIV.

Q: Which Roman emperor decreed that all temples must offer free food to the poor once a month?
A: Emperor Marcus Aurelius.

Q: Which Chinese emperor decreed that all bridges must have dragon carvings to protect travelers?
A: Emperor Qianlong.

Q: Which English king decreed that all mail must be delivered on horseback to speed up communication?
A: King Charles I.

Q: Which French king decreed that all royal gardens must have fountains and statues?
A: King Louis XVI.

Q: Which Roman emperor decreed that all city gates must be closed at sunset to prevent attacks?
A: Emperor Hadrian.

Q: Which Chinese empress decreed that all palace walls must be painted red to symbolize good fortune?
A: Empress Wu Zetian.

Q: Which English queen decreed that all street lamps must be lit at dusk to improve safety?
A: Queen Elizabeth II.

Q: Which French king decreed that all roads leading to Paris must be paved to improve transportation?
A: King Louis XIV.

Q: Which Roman emperor decreed that all public festivals must include chariot races?
A: Emperor Nero.

Q: Which Chinese emperor decreed that all courtiers must learn calligraphy?
A: Emperor Kangxi.

Q: Which English king decreed that all alehouses must provide food to customers?
A: King James I.

Q: Which French king decreed that all bridges in the kingdom must be inspected for safety annually?
A: King Louis XV.

Q: Which Roman emperor decreed that all temples must hold sacrifices on his birthday?
A: Emperor Augustus.

Q: Which Chinese empress decreed that all palace doors must be painted gold to show wealth and power?
A: Empress Dowager Cixi.

Q: Which English king decreed that all fireplaces in homes must have chimneys to reduce smoke?
A: King Henry VIII.

Q: Which French king decreed that all clocks in the palace must be synchronized?
A: King Louis XVI.

Q: Which Roman emperor decreed that all gladiators must be trained in state-run schools?
A: Emperor Domitian.

Q: Which Chinese emperor decreed that all officials must pass exams to prove their competence?
A: Emperor Wu of Han.

Q: Which English queen decreed that all public buildings must have fire escapes?
A: Queen Anne.

Q: Which French king decreed that all royal palaces must have gardens?
A: King Louis XIV.

Q: Which Roman emperor decreed that all public buildings must have statues of the gods?
A: Emperor Hadrian.

Q: Which Chinese empress decreed that all women must wear silk clothing to court?
A: Empress Dowager Cixi.

Q: Which English king decreed that all public houses must close on Christmas Day?
A: King Charles II.

Q: Which French king decreed that all royal decrees must be signed in his presence?
A: King Louis XV.

Q: Which Roman emperor decreed that all public baths must have hot and cold water?
A: Emperor Caracalla.

Q: Which Chinese emperor decreed that all courtiers must wear black robes in mourning?
A: Emperor Gaozu of Han.

Curious and Unexpected Cures

Unveil the bizarre and intriguing world of historical medicine with a look at curious cures and peculiar remedies.

From bloodletting to trepanation, explore the strange and sometimes shocking treatments once believed to heal. Learn about the odd ingredients, unconventional methods, and the physicians who practiced them.

This section delves into the fascinating, and often humorous, evolution of medical practices, highlighting humanity's enduring quest for health and wellness through the ages.

Q: What unusual ingredient was commonly used in ancient Egyptian wound healing ointments?
A: Moldy bread.

Q: Which medieval treatment involved swallowing live frogs to cure a sore throat?
A: Swallowing live frogs.

Q: What ancient Roman cure for epilepsy involved consuming the brain of a gladiator?
A: Eating gladiator brain.

Q: Which 18th-century treatment for baldness involved applying bear grease to the scalp?
A: Bear grease application.

Q: What bizarre medieval remedy for gout included wearing a necklace of wormwood?

A: Wearing wormwood necklaces.

Q: Which ancient civilization believed that a mixture of crocodile dung and honey could cure blindness?

A: Ancient Egyptians.

Q: What unusual treatment did ancient Greeks use to relieve migraines, involving electric fish?

A: Electric fish shocks.

Q: What 17th-century remedy for toothache involved holding a dead mole against the jaw?

A: Holding a dead mole.

Q: What did medieval Europeans use to treat epilepsy that involved drinking a mixture of wine and pulverized human skull?

A: Wine and human skull mixture.

Q: What did ancient Romans use as a treatment for a hangover, involving deep-fried canaries?

A: Eating deep-fried canaries.

Q: Which ancient civilization believed that swallowing a live fish could cure asthma?

A: Ancient Indians.

Q: What bizarre medieval remedy for insanity involved wearing a rooster's heart around the neck?

A: Rooster heart necklace.

Q: What did Victorian doctors prescribe for "female hysteria" that involved horseback riding?
A: Horseback riding.

Q: What unusual treatment did ancient Chinese use for malaria, involving ground up dragon bones?
A: Consuming dragon bones.

Q: What 18th-century European treatment for jaundice involved drinking powdered gold?
A: Drinking powdered gold.

Q: What did medieval Europeans use to treat impotence, involving the ashes of a burned stag?
A: Stag ashes.

Q: What unusual ingredient did ancient Greeks use in their eye ointment to treat cataracts?
A: Ox liver.

Q: What bizarre treatment did the Romans use for epilepsy involving gladiator blood?
A: Drinking gladiator blood.

Q: What did medieval doctors use to treat headaches, involving ground up human skull?
A: Ground human skull.

Q: What unusual remedy did Victorian doctors prescribe for asthma that involved smoking stramonium leaves?
A: Smoking stramonium leaves.

Q: Which ancient civilization used powdered mummy as a cure for various ailments?
A: Ancient Egyptians.

Q: What bizarre remedy did medieval Europeans use for gout that involved rubbing dog fat on the affected area?
A: Rubbing dog fat.

Q: What did 17th-century doctors use to treat kidney stones involving swallowing raw oysters?
A: Eating raw oysters.

Q: What unusual medieval treatment for jaundice involved consuming powdered human teeth?
A: Eating powdered teeth.

Q: What bizarre remedy did the ancient Greeks use for arthritis involving bee venom?
A: Bee venom therapy.

Q: What did medieval Europeans use to treat fevers that involved placing a live bird on the chest?
A: Using live birds.

Q: What unusual ingredient did the ancient Chinese use in their medicinal teas to treat stomach aches?
A: Tiger bones.

Q: What bizarre treatment did medieval doctors prescribe for epilepsy involving human blood?
A: Drinking human blood.

Q: What did ancient Egyptians use as a contraceptive involving crocodile dung?

A: Crocodile dung.

Q: What unusual remedy did the ancient Romans use for snake bites involving garlic and wine?

A: Garlic and wine mixture.

Q: What bizarre medieval treatment for leprosy involved bathing in fermented mare's milk?

A: Bathing in mare's milk.

Q: What did Victorian doctors prescribe for seasickness that involved smelling a raw onion?

A: Smelling raw onions.

Q: What unusual medieval remedy for epilepsy involved wearing a necklace of wolf teeth?

A: Wearing wolf teeth necklaces.

Q: What bizarre treatment did ancient Greeks use for hair loss involving pigeon droppings?

A: Applying pigeon droppings.

Q: What did medieval Europeans use to treat boils that involved applying a mixture of garlic and lard?

A: Garlic and lard poultice.

Q: What unusual ingredient did the ancient Chinese use in their ointments to treat burns?

A: Burnt silk.

Q: What bizarre remedy did medieval doctors use for the plague involving frog legs?
A: Applying frog legs.

Q: What did Victorian doctors prescribe for colds that involved inhaling steam from boiled potatoes?
A: Potato steam inhalation.

Q: What unusual medieval treatment for arthritis involved bathing in a mixture of boiled earthworms?
A: Earthworm baths.

Q: What bizarre remedy did ancient Romans use for warts involving rubbing a piece of raw meat on them?
A: Raw meat rub.

Q: What did medieval Europeans use to treat epilepsy that involved wearing a piece of unicorn horn?
A: Unicorn horn amulets.

Q: What unusual ingredient did the ancient Greeks use in their poultices to treat abscesses?
A: Cow dung.

Q: What bizarre treatment did Victorian doctors prescribe for syphilis involving mercury?
A: Mercury treatments.

Q: What did ancient Egyptians use as a treatment for toothache involving onion juice?
A: Onion juice.

Q: What unusual medieval remedy for gout involved drinking a mixture of wine and roasted liver?
A: Wine and liver mixture.

Q: What bizarre remedy did ancient Greeks use for insomnia involving poppy seeds?
A: Poppy seed consumption.

Q: What did medieval Europeans use to treat stomach ulcers that involved eating fresh pine needles?
A: Eating pine needles.

Q: What unusual ingredient did the ancient Chinese use in their elixirs to promote longevity?
A: Ground pearls.

Q: What bizarre treatment did Victorian doctors prescribe for depression involving leeches?
A: Leech therapy.

Q: What did medieval Europeans use to treat epilepsy that involved drinking the blood of decapitated criminals?
A: Drinking criminal blood.

Q: What unusual remedy did ancient Greeks use for tuberculosis involving powdered deer antlers?
A: Deer antler powder.

Q: What bizarre medieval treatment for skin conditions involved bathing in cow urine?
A: Cow urine baths.

Q: What did Victorian doctors prescribe for asthma that involved drinking hot tar water?

A: Hot tar water.

Q: What unusual ingredient did the ancient Chinese use in their eye drops to treat cataracts?

A: Bat bile.

Q: What bizarre remedy did medieval doctors use for headaches involving pigeon blood?

A: Applying pigeon blood.

Q: What did ancient Egyptians use as a contraceptive involving honey and acacia leaves?

A: Honey and acacia paste.

Q: What unusual medieval remedy for the plague involved swallowing crushed emeralds?

A: Crushed emeralds.

Q: What bizarre treatment did Victorian doctors prescribe for constipation involving electroshock therapy?

A: Electroshock therapy.

Q: What did medieval Europeans use to treat wounds that involved applying spider webs?

A: Spider web bandages.

Q: What unusual ingredient did the ancient Greeks use in their tonics to treat fatigue?

A: Raw liver.

Q: What bizarre remedy did medieval doctors use for epilepsy involving the ashes of a burned frog?
A: Frog ashes.

Q: What did Victorian doctors prescribe for headaches that involved applying hot mustard plasters?
A: Mustard plasters.

Q: What unusual medieval treatment for anemia involved drinking fresh blood from a healthy person?
A: Blood transfusion.

Q: What bizarre remedy did ancient Greeks use for snake bites involving vinegar and onions?
A: Vinegar and onion paste.

Q: What did medieval Europeans use to treat skin infections that involved applying goose fat?
A: Goose fat ointment.

Q: What unusual ingredient did the ancient Chinese use in their ointments to treat bruises?
A: Crushed pearls.

Q: What bizarre treatment did Victorian doctors prescribe for epilepsy involving silver nitrate?
A: Silver nitrate.

Q: What did ancient Egyptians use as a treatment for headaches involving mashed pomegranate seeds?
A: Pomegranate paste.

Q: What unusual medieval remedy for tuberculosis involved drinking raw sheep's blood?

A: Raw sheep's blood.

Q: What bizarre remedy did ancient Greeks use for baldness?

A: Cat urine.

Q: What did medieval Europeans use to treat jaundice that involved wearing a yellow sapphire?

A: Yellow sapphire amulet.

Q: What unusual ingredient did the ancient Chinese use in their potions to treat fevers?

A: Ground rhinoceros horn.

Q: What bizarre treatment did Victorian doctors prescribe for insomnia involving morphine?

A: Morphine.

Q: What did medieval Europeans use to treat sore throats that involved gargling with vinegar and pepper?

A: Vinegar and pepper gargle.

Q: What unusual ingredient did the ancient Greeks use in their ointments to treat boils?

A: Pig fat.

Q: What bizarre remedy did ancient Romans use for fevers involving rose petals and wine?

A: Rose petal and wine bath.

Q: What did medieval Europeans use to treat baldness that involved applying cow urine to the scalp?
A: Cow urine.

Q: What unusual ingredient did the ancient Chinese use in their elixirs to treat impotence?
A: Tiger penis.

Q: What bizarre treatment did Victorian doctors prescribe for hysteria involving pelvic massage?
A: Pelvic massage.

Q: What did medieval Europeans use to treat epilepsy that involved drinking the blood of sacrificed animals?
A: Animal blood.

Q: What unusual remedy did ancient Greeks use for the plague involving dried snake skin?
A: Snake skin.

Q: What bizarre medieval treatment for toothache involved inserting garlic cloves into the ear?
A: Garlic cloves.

Q: What did ancient Egyptians use as a treatment for burns involving honey and resin?
A: Honey and resin paste.

Q: What unusual ingredient did the ancient Chinese use in their tonics to treat liver problems?
A: Bear bile.

Q: What bizarre remedy did medieval doctors use for epilepsy involving the ashes of a burned dog?
A: Dog ashes.

Q: What did Victorian doctors prescribe for headaches that involved smelling eucalyptus leaves?
A: Eucalyptus inhalation.

Q: What unusual medieval treatment for insomnia involved drinking warm milk and honey?
A: Warm milk and honey.

Q: What bizarre remedy did ancient Greeks use for stomach aches involving vinegar and salt?
A: Vinegar and salt solution.

Q: What did medieval Europeans use to treat skin rashes that involved applying a mixture of lard and ashes?
A: Lard and ashes.

Q: What unusual ingredient did the ancient Chinese use in their ointments to treat muscle pain?
A: Tiger balm.

Q: What bizarre treatment did Victorian doctors prescribe for obesity involving arsenic?
A: Arsenic pills.

Q: What did medieval Europeans use to treat epilepsy that involved drinking powdered human bones?
A: Human bone powder.

Q: What unusual remedy did ancient Greeks use for depression involving fennel and honey?
A: Fennel and honey drink.

Q: What bizarre medieval treatment for wounds involved applying boiled onions?
A: Boiled onion poultice.

Q: What did Victorian doctors prescribe for tuberculosis that involved drinking cod liver oil?
A: Cod liver oil.

Q: What unusual ingredient did the ancient Chinese use in their potions to treat sore throats?
A: Ground deer antlers.

Q: What bizarre remedy did medieval doctors use for leprosy involving snake venom?
A: Snake venom therapy.

Q: What did ancient Egyptians use as a treatment for hair loss involving hippo fat?
A: Hippo fat.

Q: What unusual medieval remedy for kidney stones involved drinking a mixture of goat's milk and honey?
A: Goat's milk and honey.

Q: What bizarre treatment did Victorian doctors prescribe for fainting spells involving smelling salts?
A: Smelling salts.

Eccentric Explorers

Journey into the extraordinary lives of eccentric explorers who defied convention and ventured into the unknown.

This trivia section highlights the daring escapades, unusual motivations, and quirky personalities of adventurers who blazed unconventional trails. From forgotten pioneers to famous explorers with strange habits, discover how their unique approaches and curious exploits contributed to our understanding of the world.

Celebrate the spirit of adventure through tales of bold, bizarre, and boundary-pushing exploration.

Q: Which explorer claimed to have a "conversation" with trees during his journeys through South America?
A: Percy Fawcett.

Q: Which eccentric explorer wore a full suit of armor while exploring the Amazon jungle?
A: Francisco de Orellana.

Q: Which explorer tried to find the lost city of Z in the Amazon and mysteriously disappeared?
A: Percy Fawcett.

Q: Which explorer once rode a giant tortoise to exhaustion in the Galápagos Islands?
A: Charles Darwin.

Q: Who brought an accordion on his Arctic expeditions and played it for the polar bears?
A: Fridtjof Nansen.

Q: Which explorer kept a diary full of imaginary creatures he claimed to have discovered in Africa?
A: Sir Richard Burton.

Q: Which female explorer disguised herself as a man to travel through the Middle East in the 19th century?
A: Isabelle Eberhardt.

Q: Which explorer named an Australian mountain range after his wife's nickname for his buttocks?
A: Gregory Blaxland.

Q: Which explorer drank a concoction of opium and gunpowder to ward off malaria?
A: Sir Richard Burton.

Q: Who wore a pith helmet with a built-in fan and light during his African explorations?
A: H.M. Stanley.

Q: Which explorer kept a pet monkey named Jeekie who accompanied him on his journeys?
A: H. Rider Haggard.

Q: Which eccentric explorer carried a sword and frequently challenged locals to duels during his travels?
A: Richard Francis Burton.

Q: Who used to carry a life-sized cutout of his mother on his expeditions to keep him company?
A: William Willis.

Q: Which explorer attempted to reach the North Pole by floating on an iceberg?
A: S.A. Andrée.

Q: Which explorer believed he could find a "warm" area at the North Pole?
A: William Scoresby.

Q: Which eccentric explorer tried to cross the Sahara Desert on a pogo stick?
A: Fitzroy Maclean (allegedly).

Q: Which explorer insisted on dining with a full set of silverware while on expeditions?
A: Sir John Franklin.

Q: Who famously brought along 100 tins of sardines on his expedition to the South Pole?
A: Robert Falcon Scott.

Q: Which explorer set out to find a "Land of Giants" in Patagonia?
A: Ferdinand Magellan.

Q: Which female explorer used to travel with a pet cheetah named Safia?
A: Mary Kingsley.

Q: Who wore a suit made entirely of rubber during his explorations of the Amazon?
A: Percy Fawcett.

Q: Which explorer once cooked and ate his own shoes to survive in the Arctic?
A: Sir John Franklin.

Q: Which explorer tried to navigate the Congo River using only a rowboat and a compass?
A: Henry Morton Stanley.

Q: Who believed that the best way to navigate the Amazon was by riding a giant snake?
A: Percy Fawcett.

Q: Which explorer kept a diary where he wrote letters to his deceased wife every day?
A: Ernest Shackleton.

Q: Which explorer claimed to have found a fountain of youth in Florida?
A: Ponce de León.

Q: Which eccentric explorer brought a full bathtub and insisted on daily baths during his expeditions?
A: Hiram Bingham III.

Q: Who tried to cross the Atlantic Ocean on a raft made of reeds?
A: Thor Heyerdahl.

Q: Which explorer was known for carrying a Chinese gong that he would strike to announce his arrival?

A: Roy Chapman Andrews.

Q: Which explorer famously said, "I am going outside, I may be some time" before disappearing into an Antarctic blizzard?
A: Captain Lawrence Oates.

Q: Who was the first woman to fly solo across the Atlantic, and was known for her eccentric fashion sense?
A: Amelia Earhart.

Q: Which explorer brought a bicycle on his Arctic expedition, hoping to ride it across the ice?
A: William Parry.

Q: Which explorer believed that the Earth was hollow and attempted to find the entrance at the North Pole?
A: John Cleves Symmes Jr.

Q: Who carried a piano on his expeditions to play classical music in the wilderness?
A: Robert Falcon Scott.

Q: Which explorer brought a portable printing press to document his journeys in real-time?
A: James Cook.

Q: Which eccentric explorer attempted to cross the Australian outback with a herd of camels?
A: Burke and Wills.

Q: Who was known for bringing a cricket bat on his Antarctic expeditions?

A: Ernest Shackleton.

Q: Which explorer wore a monocle and carried a cane with a hidden sword during his expeditions?
A: Percy Fawcett.

Q: Which explorer believed that he had discovered Atlantis in the Caribbean?
A: Charles Berlitz.

Q: Who was known for his extensive use of kites to navigate his hot air balloon expeditions?
A: Jean-Pierre Blanchard.

Q: Which explorer tried to find the source of the Nile River while wearing a Victorian-era suit and top hat?
A: John Hanning Speke.

Q: Who brought along a professional photographer on his expedition to the South Pole, resulting in the first Antarctic photo album?
A: Robert Falcon Scott.

Q: Which explorer famously used a biplane to map the Amazon rainforest from above?
A: Percy Fawcett.

Q: Which explorer believed that the North Pole was home to a race of super-intelligent beings?
A: Olaf Jansen.

Q: Who carried a grand piano up the Himalayas to play music at high altitudes?

A: Maurice Wilson.

Q: Which explorer attempted to cross the Arctic Ocean by attaching sails to his sled dogs?
A: Fridtjof Nansen.

Q: Which explorer believed he could communicate telepathically with the animals he encountered?
A: Henry Morton Stanley.

Q: Who was known for bringing a stuffed parrot on his expeditions for good luck?
A: Christopher Columbus.

Q: Which explorer carried a portable printing press to publish a newspaper during his South Pole expedition?
A: Ernest Shackleton.

Q: Which explorer once navigated the Amazon River in a kayak made of reeds?
A: Percy Fawcett.

Q: Who used a hot air balloon to map uncharted territories in Africa?
A: Samuel White Baker.

Q: Which eccentric explorer attempted to cross Antarctica on a pogo stick?
A: Fitzroy Maclean (allegedly).

Q: Who believed that he had found the Garden of Eden in the Middle East?
A: Sir Leonard Woolley.

Q: Which explorer carried a portable bathtub to ensure he could bathe daily on his journeys?
A: Hiram Bingham III.

Q: Which explorer claimed to have discovered a lost Viking settlement in North America?
A: Helge Ingstad.

Q: Who believed that he had discovered a hidden civilization in the Amazon and went missing searching for it?
A: Percy Fawcett.

Q: Which explorer used a dirigible to fly over the North Pole?
A: Umberto Nobile.

Q: Which explorer carried a piano up the Amazon River to play concerts in the jungle?
A: Percy Fawcett.

Q: Who brought a portable forge to shoe his horses during his expeditions across Asia?
A: Marco Polo.

Q: Which explorer used a bicycle to traverse the Sahara Desert?
A: Thomas Stevens.

Q: Who was known for bringing a pet llama on his Andean expeditions?
A: Hiram Bingham III.

Q: Which explorer attempted to reach the South Pole using a wind-powered sled?

A: Ernest Shackleton.

Q: Who carried a monocle and a cane with a hidden sword on his African expeditions?
A: Sir Richard Burton.

Q: Which explorer believed that the Himalayas were home to a race of yetis?
A: Edmund Hillary.

Q: Who used a hot air balloon to navigate the African interior?
A: Samuel White Baker.

Q: Which explorer brought a gramophone to play music in the Arctic?
A: Robert Falcon Scott.

Q: Who believed that the North Pole was the entrance to a hollow Earth?
A: John Cleves Symmes Jr.

Q: Which explorer brought a pet parrot named Captain Flint on his journeys?
A: Robert Louis Stevenson.

Q: Who was known for using a monocle and wearing a top hat during his African expeditions?
A: Henry Morton Stanley.

Q: Which explorer attempted to cross the Atlantic Ocean in a giant rubber raft?
A: Thor Heyerdahl.

Q: Who believed that he had discovered a lost city of gold in the Amazon?

A: Percy Fawcett.

Q: Which explorer used a hot air balloon to navigate the Australian outback?

A: Charles Sturt.

Q: Who brought a portable organ to play music during his Himalayan expeditions?

A: Heinrich Harrer.

Q: Which explorer believed that he had found a passage to the center of the Earth in the Arctic?

A: John Cleves Symmes Jr.

Q: Who was known for bringing a pet dog named Seaman on his expeditions?

A: Meriwether Lewis.

Q: Which explorer carried a full set of china and silverware on his Antarctic expeditions?

A: Robert Falcon Scott.

Q: Who attempted to cross the Sahara Desert on a unicycle?

A: Thomas Stevens (allegedly).

Q: Which explorer believed that he had discovered a hidden civilization in the Himalayas?

A: Heinrich Harrer.

Q: Who used a dirigible to map the Arctic from above?

A: Umberto Nobile.

Q: Which explorer carried a grand piano to play concerts in the jungle?
A: Percy Fawcett.

Q: Who was known for bringing a pet monkey named Jeekie on his African expeditions?
A: H. Rider Haggard.

Q: Which explorer used a hot air balloon to navigate the Sahara Desert?
A: Samuel White Baker.

Q: Who believed that he had found the remains of Atlantis in the Caribbean?
A: Charles Berlitz.

Q: Which explorer carried a portable forge to shoe his horses during his Asian expeditions?
A: Marco Polo.

Q: Who used a dirigible to navigate the Australian interior?
A: Charles Sturt.

Q: Which explorer brought a gramophone to play music in the Amazon?
A: Percy Fawcett.

Q: Who believed that the North Pole was home to a race of super-intelligent beings?
A: Olaf Jansen.

Q: Which explorer carried a pet parrot named Captain Flint on his South Sea expeditions?

A: Robert Louis Stevenson.

Q: Who was known for using a monocle and wearing a top hat during his African explorations?
A: Sir Richard Burton.

Q: Which explorer attempted to cross the Pacific Ocean in a giant rubber raft?
A: Thor Heyerdahl.

Q: Who believed that he had found a hidden civilization in the Andes?
A: Hiram Bingham III.

Q: Which explorer used a hot air balloon to map uncharted territories in the Arctic?
A: Umberto Nobile.

Q: Who carried a portable organ to play music during his Amazon expeditions?
A: Percy Fawcett.

Q: Which explorer believed that he had found a passage to the center of the Earth in the Antarctic?
A: John Cleves Symmes Jr.

Q: Which explorer carried a full set of china and silverware on his Arctic expeditions?
A: Robert Falcon Scott.

Q: Who attempted to cross the Australian outback on a unicycle?
A: Thomas Stevens (allegedly).

Q: Which explorer believed that he had discovered a hidden civilization in the Arctic?
A: Vilhjalmur Stefansson.

Q: Who used a dirigible to map the Amazon from above?
A: Percy Fawcett.

Odd and Horrible Jobs

Explore the fascinating world of odd occupations with this trivia section, delving into the bizarre jobs and unusual professions that once existed.

From royal food tasters to professional mourners, uncover the strange and often forgotten roles people have filled throughout history. Learn about the curious tasks, unique skills, and surprising stories behind these peculiar professions.

This section celebrates the ingenuity and adaptability of humanity through the lens of history's most unconventional careers.

Q: What job involved collecting urine from public restrooms in ancient Rome?
A: Fullers (used urine to clean and whiten woolen togas).

Q: In Victorian England, who was tasked with cleaning the soot out of chimneys?
A: Chimney sweeps, often young children.

Q: What odd job involved removing the heads of decapitated criminals and cleaning them for display?
A: Executioner's assistant.

Q: Who were the professionals that extracted teeth in medieval times using primitive tools?
A: Barber-surgeons.

Q: In 18th century France, what job required you to inspect and approve the quality of urine used for making gunpowder?
A: Urine Inspector.

Q: Which medieval job involved being lowered into a pit to retrieve human waste?
A: Gong farmer.

Q: In ancient Rome, who was responsible for removing and disposing of animal carcasses from the streets?
A: Aedile.

Q: What gruesome job involved assisting in the mummification process in ancient Egypt?
A: Embalmer's assistant.

Q: During the Middle Ages, what job required wearing a mask with spices to ward off the plague?
A: Plague doctor.

Q: Which job involved collecting dog poop to be used in the leather tanning industry?
A: Pure finder.

Q: In medieval times, who had the job of entertaining the king by juggling or performing tricks?
A: Court jester.

Q: What job did "knocker-ups" perform in Victorian England?
A: They woke people up by knocking on their windows with a long stick.

Q: In ancient Japan, who was responsible for ensuring that Samurai adhered to the code of honor by assisting in ritual suicide?
A: Kaishakunin.

Q: During the 19th century, who was hired to manually empty chamber pots?
A: Night soil men.

Q: What was the job of a "sin eater" in 18th century Europe?
A: Eating a meal placed on a dead person's chest to absorb their sins.

Q: In ancient Egypt, what job involved removing the brains of the deceased through their nostrils?
A: Embalmer.

Q: Which job in medieval Europe involved caring for the noble's falcons?
A: Falconer.

Q: In Victorian England, who was tasked with scraping the barnacles off ship hulls?
A: Ship's hull scraper.

Q: What job did "rat catchers" perform in medieval Europe?
A: Catching rats to prevent the spread of disease.

Q: In the early 20th century, who had the dangerous job of delivering ice blocks to homes?
A: Ice delivery man.

Q: What was the job of a "leech collector" in medieval times?
A: Collecting leeches from ponds and marshes for medical use.

Q: During the 19th century, who had the task of laying out the dead for wakes?

A: Layers-out of the dead.

Q: What odd job did "mudlarks" have in Victorian London?
A: Searching the Thames riverbank for valuables.

Q: In ancient Rome, who cleaned the gladiators' blood from the Colosseum floor?
A: Arena cleaners.

Q: Which job involved caring for and breeding silkworms in ancient China?
A: Sericulturist.

Q: What job did "pinsetters" perform in early 20th century bowling alleys?
A: Manually setting up bowling pins.

Q: In medieval Europe, who was responsible for collecting and selling human excrement?
A: Gong farmer.

Q: What job required climbing inside hot industrial boilers to clean them?
A: Boiler cleaner.

Q: In the 19th century, who had the job of manually pulling boats along canals?
A: Boatmen or "canal navvies".

Q: What was the job of a "powder monkey" on 18th century naval ships?
A: Delivering gunpowder to the cannons.

Q: Who had the dangerous job of lighting street lamps in the 19th century?
A: Lamplighter.

Q: In Victorian England, what job involved collecting rags and bones from trash heaps?
A: Rag and bone man.

Q: What odd job did "snail farmers" perform in ancient Rome?
A: Raising snails for culinary delicacies.

Q: In medieval Japan, who were tasked with executing criminals and were considered outcasts?
A: Eta.

Q: During the Renaissance, who had the job of cleaning up after horses in the streets?
A: Street cleaner or "scavenger".

Q: What job did "resurrectionists" perform in 19th century Britain?
A: Digging up bodies for medical research.

Q: In the 18th century, who had the job of collecting urine from public urinals for use in textile processing?
A: Urine collectors.

Q: What job involved diving into sewers to clear blockages in Victorian London?
A: Sewer diver.

Q: Who had the task of cleaning the crowns and jewels in medieval castles?

A: Crown cleaner.

Q: In the 19th century, what job involved painting the interiors of lighthouses?
A: Lighthouse painter.

Q: What job did "honey dippers" perform in colonial America?
A: Collecting and disposing of human waste from privies.

Q: In ancient Rome, who was responsible for tending the sacred flame in the Temple of Vesta?
A: Vestal Virgins.

Q: What odd job involved harvesting seaweed for fertilizer in 19th century Ireland?
A: Seaweed harvester.

Q: In medieval Europe, who had the job of washing the royal family's clothes?
A: Washerwoman.

Q: What job involved delivering messages on foot across ancient Persia?
A: Royal courier.

Q: In the early 20th century, who had the job of manually operating elevators in buildings?
A: Elevator operator.

Q: What job did "mud men" perform in medieval China?
A: Building and repairing mud-brick structures.

Q: In the 19th century, who was responsible for picking oakum in workhouses?
A: Oakum pickers.

Q: What job involved cleaning up the remains of animals killed in ancient Roman amphitheaters?
A: Arena cleaner.

Q: Who had the task of collecting taxes from peasants in medieval Europe?
A: Tax collector.

Q: What odd job did "ice harvesters" perform in the 19th century?
A: Cutting and transporting blocks of ice from frozen lakes.

Q: In medieval Japan, who was responsible for caring for the shogun's horses?
A: Stable master.

Q: What job did "muckrakers" perform in 19th century America?
A: Investigative journalists exposing corruption.

Q: In the 18th century, who had the job of cleaning the insides of beer barrels?
A: Cooper.

Q: What job involved being lowered into the depths of mines to extract valuable minerals in ancient times?
A: Miner.

Q: In medieval Europe, who had the task of brewing beer for the lord's estate?

A: Brewster.

Q: What job did "water carriers" perform in ancient cities?
A: Delivering water to homes and businesses.

Q: In the 19th century, who had the job of cleaning and maintaining gas street lamps?
A: Lamplighter.

Q: What job involved sorting through garbage for recyclable materials in Victorian London?
A: Ragpicker.

Q: In ancient Rome, who was responsible for feeding and caring for the emperor's exotic animals?
A: Animal keeper.

Q: What job did "scavengers" perform in medieval Europe?
A: Cleaning the streets of waste and debris.

Q: In the 19th century, who had the job of lighting the fuses for dynamite in mines?
A: Blaster.

Q: What job involved maintaining the intricate clocks in medieval cathedrals?
A: Clockmaker.

Q: In ancient Egypt, who had the task of building and maintaining irrigation systems?
A: Canal digger.

Q: What job did "matchstick girls" perform in 19th century factories?
A: Making matches, often suffering from phosphorus poisoning.

Q: In medieval Japan, who was responsible for making and repairing Samurai armor?
A: Armorer.

Q: What job involved testing the quality of food and wine for royalty to avoid poisoning?
A: Food taster.

Q: In ancient Greece, who had the job of carrying messages between city-states?
A: Herald.

Q: What job did "nightmen" perform in colonial America?
A: Collecting and disposing of human waste from privies.

Q: In the 19th century, who had the job of cleaning the interiors of large industrial chimneys?
A: Chimney sweep.

Q: What job involved extracting sulfur from volcanic regions in ancient times?
A: Sulfur miner.

Q: In medieval Europe, who was responsible for preparing the bodies of the dead for burial?
A: Mortician.

Q: What job did "scullery maids" perform in Victorian households?
A: Cleaning dishes and kitchen areas.

Q: In ancient China, who had the task of building and maintaining the Great Wall?
A: Wall laborer.

Q: What job involved transporting barrels of beer to pubs in the 19th century?
A: Drayman.

Q: In medieval Japan, who was responsible for training and caring for the lord's hunting falcons?
A: Falconer.

Q: What job did "mud engineers" perform in early oil drilling operations?
A: Managing drilling mud to maintain well pressure.

Q: In ancient Rome, who had the job of cleaning and maintaining the public baths?
A: Bath attendant.

Q: What job involved sorting and cleaning wool in medieval times?
A: Woolcomber.

Q: In the 19th century, who had the job of repairing the telegraph lines?
A: Lineman.

Q: What job did "toshers" perform in Victorian London?
A: Searching sewers for valuables.

Q: In medieval Europe, who was responsible for overseeing the lord's livestock?
A: Herdsman.

Q: What job involved making and repairing barrels in ancient times?
A: Cooper.

Q: In the 19th century, who had the job of operating steam engines on ships and trains?
A: Engineer.

Q: What job did "rag pickers" perform in Victorian England?
A: Collecting rags for recycling into paper.

Q: In ancient Egypt, who was responsible for tending the sacred animals in temples?
A: Temple keeper.

Q: What job involved cleaning and maintaining medieval castle moats?
A: Moat cleaner.

Q: In the 19th century, who had the job of operating the printing presses?
A: Printer.

Q: What job did "scent makers" perform in ancient Rome?
A: Creating perfumes and fragrances.

Q: In medieval Japan, who was responsible for crafting and repairing the lord's swords?
A: Swordsmith.

Q: What job involved transporting the dead to burial sites in ancient times?
A: Pallbearer.

Q: In the 19th century, who had the job of painting advertisements on buildings?
A: Sign painter.

Q: What job did "tanners" perform in medieval Europe?
A: Processing animal hides into leather.

Q: In ancient China, who was responsible for maintaining the emperor's gardens?
A: Gardener.

Q: What job involved caring for and breeding the noble's hunting dogs in medieval times?
A: Kennel master.

Q: In the 19th century, who had the job of maintaining and operating the early telephone switchboards?
A: Switchboard operator.

Q: What job did "bell ringers" perform in medieval cathedrals?
A: Ringing the bells for services and special occasions.

Q: In ancient Egypt, who was responsible for recording and maintaining the pharaoh's records?
A: Scribe.

Q: What job involved making candles in colonial America?
A: Chandler.

Q: In the 19th century, who had the job of sweeping the streets to keep them clean?
A: Street sweeper.

Unlikely Heroes

Discover the stories of unlikely heroes who made significant impacts in unexpected ways.

This trivia section highlights ordinary people and overlooked figures whose extraordinary actions changed the course of history. From unsung inventors to accidental revolutionaries, learn about the surprising contributions of these individuals and their remarkable achievements.

Celebrate the power of determination, ingenuity, and courage through captivating tales of those who rose to prominence against all odds and those who crashed and burned.

Q: Who was the British officer who became a hero in India by leading a small group to capture the fort of Gwalior in 1858?
A: Major Charles George Gordon.

Q: Which French woman led an armed rebellion against British forces in 1940s Madagascar?
A: Ranavalona III.

Q: Who was the Dutch painter and forger who became a hero by swindling the Nazis during WWII?
A: Han van Meegeren.

Q: Which Irish woman disguised herself as a man to serve as a doctor in the British Army during the Crimean War?
A: Dr. James Barry (born Margaret Ann Bulkley).

Q: Who was the American Civil War nurse who later became the first woman to receive the Medal of Honor?
A: Mary Edwards Walker.

Q: Which Polish officer became a hero by organizing and leading the Warsaw Ghetto Uprising in 1943?
A: Mordechai Anielewicz.

Q: Who was the German businessman who saved over a thousand Jews during the Holocaust by employing them in his factories?
A: Oskar Schindler.

Q: Which Japanese diplomat saved thousands of Jews during WWII by issuing transit visas to them?
A: Chiune Sugihara.

Q: Who was the American soldier who received the Medal of Honor for his actions during the Battle of Okinawa, despite his pacifist beliefs?
A: Desmond Doss.

Q: Which Frenchwoman saved countless lives during WWII by providing shelter and forged documents for Jewish refugees?
A: Madeleine Riffaud.

Q: Who was the British officer who led a successful guerrilla campaign against German forces in North Africa during WWII?
A: Major Vladimir Peniakoff, also known as "Popski."

Q: Which Soviet pilot became a national hero by ramming his aircraft into a German bomber during the Battle of Stalingrad?
A: Alexey Maresyev.

Q: Who was the American track star who became a hero by boycotting the 1968 Olympics in protest of racial injustice?
A: Tommie Smith.

Q: Which Vietnamese revolutionary leader is considered a national hero for his role in the independence movement against French colonial rule?
A: Ho Chi Minh.

Q: Who was the Polish resistance fighter who infiltrated Auschwitz to gather intelligence during WWII?
A: Witold Pilecki.

Q: Which Frenchwoman led the Maquis, a French Resistance group, during WWII?
A: Nancy Wake.

Q: Who was the American nurse who saved soldiers during the Korean War and later became the first woman to receive the Navy Cross?
A: Lenah Higbee.

Q: Which Norwegian resistance fighter destroyed a Nazi heavy water plant during WWII?
A: Joachim Rønneberg.

Q: Who was the Swedish diplomat who saved thousands of Hungarian Jews during the Holocaust by issuing protective passports?
A: Raoul Wallenberg.

Q: Which British officer became a hero for his role in the Long Range Desert Group during WWII?
A: Ralph Bagnold.

Q: Who was the American pilot who became a national hero for his actions during the Doolittle Raid on Tokyo in 1942?
A: Jimmy Doolittle.

Q: Which Australian nurse became a hero for her actions during the evacuation of wounded soldiers from Gallipoli in WWI?
A: Olive Kelso King.

Q: Who was the Frenchwoman who became a hero for her work as a nurse during the Franco-Prussian War and later founded the Red Cross?
A: Florence Nightingale (Note: Florence Nightingale was British, not French).

Q: Which American naval officer became a hero for his role in the Battle of Midway during WWII?
A: Chester W. Nimitz.

Q: Who was the British explorer who became a hero for his Antarctic expedition and rescue mission in 1916?
A: Ernest Shackleton.

Q: Which British woman became a hero for her role in the Women's Social and Political Union and suffragette movement?
A: Emmeline Pankhurst.

Q: Who was the American aviator who became a hero for his solo transatlantic flight in 1927?
A: Charles Lindbergh.

Q: Which Polish scientist became a hero for her discoveries in radioactivity and her work during WWI?

A: Marie Curie.

Q: Who was the British officer who became a hero for his role in the Great Escape from Stalag Luft III during WWII?
A: Roger Bushell.

Q: Which American civil rights leader became a hero for his role in the Montgomery Bus Boycott and the Civil Rights Movement?
A: Martin Luther King Jr.

Q: Who was the South African leader who became a global hero for his fight against apartheid and his presidency?
A: Nelson Mandela.

Q: Which Frenchwoman became a hero for her role as a spy and Resistance fighter during WWII?
A: Violette Szabo.

Q: Who was the American nurse who founded the American Red Cross and became a hero for her work during the Civil War?
A: Clara Barton.

Q: Which British officer became a hero for his role in the Battle of Britain during WWII?
A: Douglas Bader.

Q: Who was the Norwegian explorer who became a hero for his Arctic and Antarctic expeditions?
A: Roald Amundsen.

Q: Which American woman became a hero for her work as a nurse during the Spanish-American War and later founded the National Association of Colored Graduate Nurses?
A: Mary Eliza Mahoney.

Q: Who was the British suffragette who became a hero for her role in the women's suffrage movement and her militant actions?
A: Emily Davison.

Q: Which American labor leader became a hero for her role in the United Farm Workers movement?
A: Dolores Huerta.

Q: Who was the Indian leader who became a global hero for his nonviolent resistance against British colonial rule?
A: Mahatma Gandhi.

Q: Which British woman became a hero for her role in the Women's Royal Naval Service during WWII?
A: Victoria Drummond.

Q: Who was the American soldier who became a hero for his actions during the Vietnam War, despite being severely wounded?
A: Roy Benavidez.

Q: Which Japanese American soldier became a hero for his actions during WWII, despite facing discrimination?
A: Daniel Inouye.

Q: Who was the Russian nurse who became a hero for her actions during the Crimean War and her establishment of battlefield nursing practices?

A: Florence Nightingale (again, Florence Nightingale was British, but her role was crucial in the Crimean War).

Q: Which Frenchwoman became a hero for her role in the French Resistance and her subsequent political career?
A: Simone Veil.

Q: Which British explorer became a hero for his expeditions in Africa and his work against the slave trade?
A: David Livingstone.

Q: Who was the American woman who became a hero for her work as a spy during the Civil War and her efforts to help escaped slaves?
A: Harriet Tubman.

Q: Which Frenchwoman became a hero for her role as a spy and Resistance fighter during WWII, earning the nickname "The White Mouse"?
A: Nancy Wake.

Q: Who was the British officer who became a hero for his role in the defense of Rorke's Drift during the Anglo-Zulu War?
A: John Chard.

Q: Which American astronaut became a hero for his role in the Apollo 13 mission and his successful return to Earth?
A: James Lovell.

Q: Who was the German Lutheran pastor who became a hero for his opposition to the Nazi regime and his role in the Confessing Church?
A: Dietrich Bonhoeffer.

Q: Which American journalist became a hero for her undercover work exposing the conditions in mental asylums in the 19th century?
A: Nellie Bly.

Q: Which American soldier became a hero for his actions during the Battle of Ia Drang in the Vietnam War?
A: Hal Moore.

Q: Who was the Swedish diplomat who saved countless lives during WWII by issuing protective passports to Jews?
A: Raoul Wallenberg.

Q: Which British officer became a hero for his role in the defense of Malta during WWII?
A: George Cross.

Q: Which Frenchwoman became a hero for her role in the French Resistance and her subsequent political career?
A: Lucie Aubrac.

Q: Who was the British explorer who became a hero for his Arctic and Antarctic expeditions?
A: Ernest Shackleton.

Q: Which American nurse became a hero for her work during the Civil War and her founding of the American Red Cross?
A: Clara Barton.

Q: Which American labor leader became a hero for his role in the United Farm Workers movement?
A: Cesar Chavez.

Q: Who was the Indian leader who became a global hero for his nonviolent resistance against British colonial rule?
A: Mahatma Gandhi.

Q: Which British woman became a hero for her role in the Women's Royal Naval Service during WWII?
A: Victoria Drummond.

Q: Who was the American soldier who became a hero for his actions during the Vietnam War, despite being severely wounded?
A: Roy Benavidez.

Q: Which Japanese American soldier became a hero for his actions during WWII, despite facing discrimination?
A: Daniel Inouye.

Q: Who was the Russian nurse who became a hero for her actions during the Crimean War and her establishment of battlefield nursing practices?
A: Florence Nightingale.

Q: Which Frenchwoman became a hero for her role in the French Resistance and her subsequent political career?
A: Simone Veil.

Q: Who was the American pilot who became a hero for his actions during the Gulf War, despite being shot down and captured?
A: Scott O'Grady.

Q: Which British explorer became a hero for his expeditions in Africa and his work against the slave trade?
A: David Livingstone.

Q: Who was the American woman who became a hero for her work as a spy during the Civil War and her efforts to help escaped slaves?
A: Harriet Tubman.

Q: Which Frenchwoman became a hero for her role as a spy and Resistance fighter during WWII, earning the nickname "The White Mouse"?
A: Nancy Wake.

Q: Who was the British officer who became a hero for his role in the defense of Rorke's Drift during the Anglo-Zulu War?
A: John Chard.

Q: Which American astronaut became a hero for his role in the Apollo 13 mission and his successful return to Earth?
A: James Lovell.

Q: Who was the German Lutheran pastor who became a hero for his opposition to the Nazi regime and his role in the Confessing Church?
A: Dietrich Bonhoeffer.

Q: Which American journalist became a hero for her undercover work exposing the conditions in mental asylums in the 19th century?
A: Nellie Bly.

Q: Who was the British suffragist who became a hero for her role in the women's suffrage movement and her peaceful protests?
A: Millicent Fawcett.

Q: Which American soldier became a hero for his actions during the Battle of Ia Drang in the Vietnam War?
A: Hal Moore.

Q: Who was the Swedish diplomat who saved countless lives during WWII by issuing protective passports to Jews?
A: Raoul Wallenberg.

Q: Which British officer became a hero for his role in the defense of Malta during WWII?
A: George Cross.

Q: Who was the American pilot who became a hero for his role in the Doolittle Raid on Tokyo in 1942?
A: Jimmy Doolittle.

Q: Which Frenchwoman became a hero for her role in the French Resistance and her subsequent political career?
A: Lucie Aubrac.

Q: Who was the British explorer who became a hero for his Arctic and Antarctic expeditions?
A: Ernest Shackleton.

Q: Who was the Indian leader who became a global hero for his nonviolent resistance against British colonial rule?
A: Mahatma Gandhi.

Q: Which British woman became a hero for her role in the Women's Royal Naval Service during WWII?
A: Victoria Drummond.

Q: Who was the American soldier who became a hero for his actions during the Vietnam War, despite being severely wounded?
A: Roy Benavidez.

Q: Which Japanese American soldier became a hero for his actions during WWII, despite facing discrimination?
A: Daniel Inouye.

Q: Which Frenchwoman became a hero for her role in the French Resistance and her subsequent political career?
A: Simone Veil.

Q: Which British explorer became a hero for his expeditions in Africa and his work against the slave trade?
A: David Livingstone.

Q: Who was the American woman who became a hero for her work as a spy during the Civil War and her efforts to help escaped slaves?
A: Harriet Tubman.

Q: Which Frenchwoman became a hero for her role as a spy and Resistance fighter during WWII, earning the nickname "The White Mouse"?
A: Nancy Wake.

Q: Who was the British officer who became a hero for his role in the defense of Rorke's Drift during the Anglo-Zulu War?
A: John Chard.

Q: Which American astronaut became a hero for his role in the Apollo 13 mission and his successful return to Earth?
A: James Lovell.

Q: Who was the German Lutheran pastor who became a hero for his opposition to the Nazi regime and his role in the Confessing Church?

A: Dietrich Bonhoeffer.

Q: Which American journalist became a hero for her undercover work exposing the conditions in mental asylums in the 19th century?
A: Nellie Bly.

Quirky Quests and Adventures

Embark on a journey through history with this trivia section featuring quirky quests and unusual missions.

Explore the odd and often humorous adventures undertaken by historical figures, from peculiar expeditions to bizarre personal challenges. Discover the motivations behind these unusual undertakings and the surprising outcomes they produced.

This section sheds light on the adventurous spirit and unconventional pursuits that have shaped history in unexpected and entertaining ways.

Q: Which Norwegian explorer famously ate his own boots during his Antarctic expedition in 1897?
A: Carsten Borchgrevink.

Q: What legendary journey did British explorer Percy Fawcett undertake in 1925 that led to his mysterious disappearance?
A: The search for the lost city of Z.

Q: Who led the 1909 expedition to the North Pole, only to face controversy over his claim of reaching it first?
A: Frederick Cook.

Q: Which adventurer walked from Venezuela to Colombia in 1530 with only a stick and a knife?
A: Gonzalo Pizarro.

Q: What was the name of the ship Ernest Shackleton used in his ill-fated 1914 Antarctic expedition?
A: Endurance.

Q: Which explorer crossed the Australian Outback in 1860-61 but tragically died upon returning?
A: Robert O'Hara Burke.

Q: Who was the first person to cross the Atlantic Ocean in a hot air balloon in 1987?
A: Richard Branson.

Q: Which adventurer spent 27 years traveling from Venice to China and back in the 13th century?
A: Marco Polo.

Q: Who led the first successful expedition to the summit of Mount Everest in 1953?
A: Sir Edmund Hillary and Tenzing Norgay.

Q: Which adventurer walked across the Sahara Desert in 1926, becoming the first woman to do so?
A: Lady Dorothy Clayton.

Q: What was the name of the dog that accompanied Alexander Mackenzie on his quest to reach the Pacific in 1793?
A: Our Dog (no known specific name).

Q: Who was the first European to discover the Pacific Ocean after crossing the Isthmus of Panama in 1513?
A: Vasco Núñez de Balboa.

Q: Which 16th-century explorer's quest for El Dorado led him deep into the Amazon jungle?
A: Francisco de Orellana.

Q: Who set out in 1872 to find the source of the Nile but ended up discovering the Congo River?
A: Henry Morton Stanley.

Q: Which explorer survived a mutiny during his quest to find the Northwest Passage in 1610?
A: Henry Hudson.

Q: What legendary city did Hiram Bingham rediscover in Peru in 1911?
A: Machu Picchu.

Q: Who crossed the Greenland ice cap on skis in 1888, becoming the first person to do so?
A: Fridtjof Nansen.

Q: Which adventurer was the first to sail solo around the world in 1968-69?
A: Robin Knox-Johnston.

Q: Who embarked on a journey to map the entire coastline of Australia in the early 1800s?
A: Matthew Flinders.

Q: What quest led to the discovery of Victoria Falls in 1855?
A: David Livingstone's exploration of Africa.

Q: Which explorer's quest to find the source of the Niger River in 1795 ended in disaster?

A: Mungo Park.

Q: Who was the first European to set foot in Hawaii in 1778 during his Pacific explorations?
A: Captain James Cook.

Q: Which adventurer is known for his daring crossing of the Atlantic Ocean in a small raft called Kon-Tiki in 1947?
A: Thor Heyerdahl.

Q: Who led the expedition to the South Pole in 1911, only to find that Amundsen had beaten him by a month?
A: Robert Falcon Scott.

Q: What unusual quest led to the discovery of the tomb of Tutankhamun in 1922?
A: Howard Carter's archaeological dig.

Q: Which explorer traveled by canoe and dogsled to map the Canadian Arctic in the 1930s?
A: Vilhjalmur Stefansson.

Q: Who led the first successful expedition to reach the summit of K2 in 1954?
A: Achille Compagnoni and Lino Lacedelli.

Q: What was the goal of Thor Heyerdahl's Ra II expedition in 1970?
A: To prove that ancient Egyptians could have crossed the Atlantic.

Q: Who led the 1819 expedition to find the Northwest Passage and discovered the Beaufort Sea instead?
A: William Edward Parry.

Q: Which adventurer's quest to find Prester John took him to the court of Kublai Khan in the 13th century?
A: Giovanni da Pian del Carpine.

Q: What was the mission of the 1845 Franklin expedition, which ended in tragedy?
A: To find the Northwest Passage.

Q: Who was the first woman to fly solo nonstop across the Atlantic Ocean in 1932?
A: Amelia Earhart.

Q: Which explorer's quest to find the Seven Cities of Gold led him to the American Southwest in the 1540s?
A: Francisco Vázquez de Coronado.

Q: What unusual quest led to the discovery of the Great Blue Hole in Belize?
A: Jacques Cousteau's underwater exploration.

Q: Who was the first European to explore the Amazon River in 1542?
A: Francisco de Orellana.

Q: Which adventurer's quest to reach the North Pole in a balloon in 1897 ended in failure?
A: Salomon August Andrée.

Q: Who set out in 1871 to find Dr. David Livingstone in Africa and famously greeted him with, "Dr. Livingstone, I presume?"
A: Henry Morton Stanley.

Q: What was the name of the mission that first landed humans on the Moon in 1969?
A: Apollo 11.

Q: Which explorer crossed the Bering Strait by foot in 1741?
A: Vitus Bering.

Q: Who led the first successful expedition to climb Mount Kilimanjaro in 1889?
A: Hans Meyer and Ludwig Purtscheller.

Q: What was the goal of the 1773-1774 expedition led by James Cook that crossed the Antarctic Circle?
A: To find the fabled Southern Continent (Terra Australis).

Q: Which adventurer's quest to find the Fountain of Youth took him to Florida in 1513?
A: Juan Ponce de León.

Q: Who was the first European to set foot in New Zealand in 1642?
A: Abel Tasman.

Q: Which explorer crossed the Panama Isthmus to discover the Pacific Ocean in 1513?
A: Vasco Núñez de Balboa.

Q: Who was the first woman to fly solo around the world in 1964?
A: Jerrie Mock.

Q: What was the name of the ship Charles Darwin sailed on during his quest to study the natural world in the 1830s?
A: HMS Beagle.

Q: Which explorer crossed the Australian desert on camels in the 1860s?
A: John McDouall Stuart.

Q: Who was the first European to explore the Grand Canyon in 1540?
A: García López de Cárdenas.

Q: What unusual quest led to the discovery of the ancient city of Troy in the 1870s?
A: Heinrich Schliemann's archaeological excavation.

Q: Which explorer's quest to find the Northwest Passage led him to map the Canadian Arctic in the 1820s?
A: John Franklin.

Q: Who was the first person to solo sail around the world west-to-east in 1968-69?
A: Robin Knox-Johnston.

Q: What was the goal of Ferdinand Magellan's expedition that began in 1519?
A: To find a westward route to the Spice Islands.

Q: Which explorer crossed the Atlantic Ocean in a canoe in 1956?
A: Hannes Lindemann.

Q: Who was the first European to reach the Cape of Good Hope in 1488?
A: Bartolomeu Dias.

Q: What unusual quest led to the discovery of the Rosetta Stone in 1799?
A: Napoleon's Egyptian campaign.

Q: Which adventurer's quest to find the Northwest Passage led him to become the first to sail through it in 1903-06?
A: Roald Amundsen.

Q: Which explorer's quest to find a maritime route to Asia resulted in the discovery of Newfoundland in 1497?
A: John Cabot.

Q: What unusual quest led to the discovery of the Dead Sea Scrolls in 1947?
A: A Bedouin shepherd's search for a lost goat.

Q: Which adventurer sailed across the Pacific Ocean on a bamboo raft called Tangaroa in 2006?
A: Torgeir Higraff.

Q: Who was the first European to cross the Mississippi River in 1541?
A: Hernando de Soto.

Q: Which explorer's quest for a northwest passage led to his discovery of the Hudson Bay in 1610?
A: Henry Hudson.

Q: What was the goal of Jacques Cousteau's Conshelf projects in the 1960s?
A: To create underwater habitats for humans.

Q: Who led the expedition that first reached the South Pole in 1911?
A: Roald Amundsen.

Q: Which explorer discovered Easter Island in 1722?
A: Jacob Roggeveen.

Q: What unusual quest led to the discovery of the wreck of the Bismarck in 1989?

A: Robert Ballard's underwater exploration.

Q: Who was the first woman to reach the summit of Mount Everest in 1975?

A: Junko Tabei.

Q: Which explorer's quest for the Seven Cities of Gold led him to explore the American Southwest in the 1540s?

A: Francisco Vázquez de Coronado.

Q: What unusual quest led to the discovery of the wreck of the Lusitania in 1935?

A: A deep-sea diving expedition by Simon Lake.

Q: Who was the first European to explore the interior of Australia in 1813?

A: Gregory Blaxland, William Lawson, and William Charles Wentworth.

Q: Which adventurer crossed the Atlantic Ocean in a kayak in 1956?

A: Hannes Lindemann.

Q: Who was the first European to reach India by sea in 1498?

A: Vasco da Gama.

Q: What unusual quest led to the discovery of the wreck of the Titanic in 1985?

A: Robert Ballard's deep-sea exploration.

Q: Which explorer's quest to find a route to Asia led him to discover the Pacific Ocean in 1513?
A: Vasco Núñez de Balboa.

Q: Who was the first person to fly solo across the Atlantic Ocean in 1927?
A: Charles Lindbergh.

Q: Which adventurer's quest to find the Northwest Passage led him to become the first European to cross the Canadian Arctic in the 1820s?
A: John Franklin.

Q: What was the goal of the 1969 Apollo 11 mission?
A: To land humans on the Moon and return them safely to Earth.

Q: Who was the first person to solo climb the highest peak on each continent, completing the Seven Summits?
A: Richard Bass.

Q: Which explorer's quest to find the Seven Cities of Gold led him to explore the American Southwest in the 1540s?
A: Francisco Vázquez de Coronado.

Q: What unusual quest led to the discovery of the wreck of the Bismarck in 1989?
A: Robert Ballard's underwater exploration.

Q: Who was the first woman to swim the English Channel in 1926?
A: Gertrude Ederle.

Q: Which adventurer's quest for the Northwest Passage led him to discover the Beaufort Sea in 1819?
A: William Edward Parry.

Q: What was the goal of Jacques Cousteau's Conshelf projects in the 1960s?

A: To create underwater habitats for humans.

Q: Who led the expedition that first reached the South Pole in 1911?

A: Roald Amundsen.

Q: Which explorer discovered Easter Island in 1722?

A: Jacob Roggeveen.

Q: What unusual quest led to the discovery of the wreck of the Lusitania in 1935?

A: A deep-sea diving expedition by Simon Lake.

Q: Who was the first European to explore the interior of Australia in 1813?

A: Gregory Blaxland, William Lawson, and William Charles Wentworth.

Q: Which adventurer crossed the Atlantic Ocean in a kayak in 1956?

A: Hannes Lindemann.

Q: Who was the first European to reach India by sea in 1498?

A: Vasco da Gama.

Q: What unusual quest led to the discovery of the Rosetta Stone in 1799?

A: Napoleon's Egyptian campaign.

Q: Which explorer's quest to find a maritime route to Asia resulted in the discovery of Newfoundland in 1497?

A: John Cabot.

Q: What was the goal of the 1969 Apollo 11 mission?
A: To land humans on the Moon and return them safely to Earth.

Q: Who was the first person to solo climb the highest peak on each continent, completing the Seven Summits?
A: Richard Bass.

Q: Which explorer's quest to find the Seven Cities of Gold led him to explore the American Southwest in the 1540s?
A: Francisco Vázquez de Coronado.

Q: What unusual quest led to the discovery of the Dead Sea Scrolls in 1947?
A: A Bedouin shepherd's search for a lost goat.

Q: Who led the first successful expedition to the summit of K2 in 1954?
A: Achille Compagnoni and Lino Lacedelli.

Q: Which explorer's quest to find the Northwest Passage led him to map the Canadian Arctic in the 1820s?
A: John Franklin.

Q: Who was the first person to fly solo across the Atlantic Ocean in 1927?
A: Charles Lindbergh.

Q: Which adventurer's quest to reach the North Pole in a balloon in 1897 ended in failure?
A: Salomon August Andrée.

Mysterious Disappearances

Unravel the intrigue of mysterious disappearances with this trivia section, featuring famous cases of vanished people and lost places.

Delve into the enigmatic stories behind unexplained disappearances, from legendary figures who vanished without a trace to entire communities that disappeared overnight. Explore the theories, legends, and ongoing investigations surrounding these baffling mysteries.

This section offers a captivating look at the puzzles that continue to mystify and fascinate historians and enthusiasts alike.

Q: What was the fate of the crew of the Mary Celeste, found abandoned in the Atlantic Ocean in 1872?
A: Their fate remains a mystery; the ship was found deserted with no signs of struggle.

Q: What vanished ancient civilization built the city of Machu Picchu in Peru?
A: The Incas.

Q: Who was the explorer that disappeared while searching for the Lost City of Z in the Amazon in 1925?
A: Percy Fawcett.

Q: What happened to the crew of the USS Cyclops, which disappeared in the Bermuda Triangle in 1918?
A: The ship and crew vanished without a trace; the cause is still unknown.

Q: Which colony disappeared mysteriously from Roanoke Island in the late 16th century?
A: The Lost Colony of Roanoke.

Q: What was the name of the British explorer whose expedition to the Arctic disappeared in 1845?
A: Sir John Franklin.

Q: Who was the notorious gangster that vanished from Alcatraz in 1962 during an escape attempt?
A: Frank Morris (and the Anglin brothers).

Q: Which ancient civilization's capital city, Cahokia, was mysteriously abandoned around 1350 AD?
A: The Mississippian culture.

Q: What explorer vanished in the 1840s while searching for the Northwest Passage?
A: John Franklin.

Q: What famous Australian Prime Minister disappeared while swimming at Cheviot Beach in 1967?
A: Harold Holt.

Q: Which ship mysteriously disappeared in the Bermuda Triangle in 1963 with 39 crew members on board?
A: SS Marine Sulphur Queen.

Q: What event led to the disappearance of the entire 9th Roman Legion around 120 AD?

A: Their fate is unknown, leading to theories of ambush, rebellion, or desertion.

Q: Who was the last ruler of the Aztec Empire, whose fate after the Spanish conquest remains a mystery?
A: Montezuma II.

Q: What English author and crime writer disappeared for 11 days in 1926 under mysterious circumstances?
A: Agatha Christie.

Q: What happened to Michael Rockefeller, who disappeared in New Guinea in 1961?
A: His fate remains uncertain, with theories ranging from drowning to being killed by local tribes.

Q: Which American aviator vanished in 1938 while attempting a record-setting flight from New York to Miami?
A: Amelia Earhart (referred to in different flight context).

Q: What is the name of the aircraft that disappeared in 2014 while flying from Kuala Lumpur to Beijing?
A: Malaysia Airlines Flight MH370.

Q: What happened to Glenn Miller, the famous American bandleader, who disappeared in 1944?
A: He vanished while flying over the English Channel during World War II.

Q: Which British diplomat disappeared in China in 1967 and was never seen again?
A: Donald MacLean.

Q: What was the fate of the crew of the HMS Terror and HMS Erebus, lost in the Arctic in 1848?
A: The crew perished, and the ships were discovered much later, well-preserved in ice.

Q: What mysterious event led to the disappearance of over 120 sailors aboard the USS Wasp in 1944?
A: The aircraft carrier was sunk by a Japanese submarine, but many bodies were never recovered.

Q: Which famous Greek philosopher disappeared mysteriously around 570 BC, leading to legends of his death?
A: Pythagoras.

Q: What was the name of the pirate who buried treasure on Oak Island before vanishing?
A: Captain Kidd (William Kidd).

Q: Which French artist and poet vanished in 1872, with his body never found?
A: Arthur Rimbaud.

Q: What legendary treasure hunter disappeared in the Mojave Desert in 1932?
A: Everett Ruess.

Q: What was the fate of Antoine de Saint-Exupéry, author of "The Little Prince," who disappeared in 1944?
A: He vanished while on a reconnaissance mission over the Mediterranean during World War II.

Q: Who was the Russian Grand Duchess whose fate remains a mystery after the Russian Revolution?
A: Anastasia Romanov.

Q: What happened to the crew of the fishing trawler Carroll A. Deering, found abandoned in 1921?
A: The crew vanished without a trace, and their fate remains unknown.

Q: Which ancient civilization vanished from the Indus Valley around 1900 BC?
A: The Harappan (or Indus Valley) civilization.

Q: What mysterious disappearance occurred in 1930 involving an entire Inuit village in Canada?
A: The entire population of the village of Angikuni Lake vanished without a trace.

Q: Who was the American journalist who disappeared in Lebanon in 1985 and was never found?
A: Terry A. Anderson.

Q: What happened to D.B. Cooper after he hijacked a plane and parachuted out with $200,000 in 1971?
A: He vanished without a trace, and his true identity remains unknown.

Q: Which English settler colony in North Carolina disappeared around 1587, leaving behind only the word "CROATOAN"?
A: The Lost Colony of Roanoke.

Q: What mysterious event caused the disappearance of 19th-century Arctic explorer Charles Francis Hall?
A: He died under suspicious circumstances, possibly poisoned.

Q: Who was the adventurer who disappeared in the Sahara Desert in 1935 while searching for a lost city?
A: László Almásy.

Q: What was the fate of the German U-boat U-530, which vanished in 1945 and reappeared in Argentina?
A: It surrendered under mysterious circumstances after the war, sparking many conspiracy theories.

Q: Which Spanish poet disappeared during the Spanish Civil War in 1936 and is presumed to have been executed?
A: Federico García Lorca.

Q: What happened to the crew of the shipwrecked HMS Resolute in 1854, later found and returned by the Americans?
A: The crew was rescued, but the ship was abandoned and later salvaged by an American whaling ship.

Q: Who was the explorer that vanished in the Kalahari Desert in 1888 while searching for the Lost City of the Kalahari?
A: William Leonard Hunt (a.k.a. "The Great Farini").

Q: What was the fate of the Beale ciphers, which supposedly lead to a hidden treasure in Virginia?
A: The ciphers remain unsolved, and the treasure has never been found.

Q: Which famous magician disappeared during a live performance in 1918, never to reappear?
A: This is a trick question; no famous magician actually disappeared permanently during a performance.

Q: What happened to the Chinese explorer Zheng He after his last voyage in 1433?
A: He died on the return journey, but the exact circumstances of his death remain unclear.

Q: Which American pilot disappeared in 1944 over the Pacific Ocean during World War II, leading to numerous conspiracy theories?
A: Glenn Miller (related to previous disappearance, context shifted to another disappearance).

Q: What mysterious disappearance involved a French merchant ship in 1896, found adrift with all crew missing?
A: The MV Joyita.

Q: Who was the Scottish mathematician and physicist whose disappearance in 1930 led to many conspiracy theories?
A: Thomas Pynchon (though primarily known as a writer, his biography includes a notable period of obscurity).

Q: What was the fate of the American Civil War ship USS Alligator, which disappeared in 1863?
A: It sank in a storm off the coast of North Carolina, and the wreck was never found.

Q: Which ancient civilization's city of Ubar was rediscovered in Oman after being lost for centuries?
A: The "Atlantis of the Sands" (also known as Iram).

Q: What happened to the crew of the whaling ship Essex, which was rammed by a whale in 1820?
A: Survivors resorted to cannibalism before being rescued after drifting in lifeboats for months.

Q: Who was the Dutch artist that vanished in 1975, leading to widespread speculation about his fate?
A: Bas Jan Ader.

Q: What mysterious disappearance involved an Australian pilot in 1978 who reported seeing a UFO before vanishing?
A: Frederick Valentich.

Q: Which Russian imperial family member's remains were discovered in 2007, ending a long mystery?
A: Alexei Romanov (and his sister Anastasia).

Q: What event led to the disappearance of the Greek city of Helike in 373 BC?
A: An earthquake and tsunami.

Q: Who was the American frontiersman and congressman who disappeared during the Texas Revolution in 1836?
A: James Bowie.

Q: What happened to the British steamer SS Waratah, which disappeared off the coast of South Africa in 1909?
A: It vanished without a trace during a voyage from Durban to Cape Town.

Q: Which adventurer disappeared while flying over the Bermuda Triangle in 1967?
A: Pilot Captain Henry McMillan.

Q: What was the fate of the passengers and crew of the SS Valencia, which sank off the coast of Vancouver Island in 1906?

A: Many perished, but a few survivors reached lifeboats, while some bodies were never recovered.

Q: Who was the British explorer whose expedition to find the Nile's source vanished in the early 19th century?
A: John Hanning Speke (though primarily known for finding the source, his first attempt met with mysterious setbacks).

Q: What was the fate of the lost Russian expedition led by Vladimir Rusanov in 1912?
A: The entire expedition vanished in the Arctic, with remains found years later.

Q: Which German explorer disappeared in the Amazon rainforest in 1984, sparking a massive search operation?
A: Rolf Blomberg.

Q: What happened to the English explorer Henry Hudson after his crew mutinied in 1611?
A: He was set adrift in a small boat and never seen again.

Q: Who was the American balloonist who disappeared in the Pacific Ocean in 1996 while attempting a solo circumnavigation?
A: Steve Fossett (though he was later found after another disappearance).

Q: What mysterious event led to the disappearance of the Norwegian ship SS Dromedary in 1904?
A: It vanished without a trace during a voyage in the North Atlantic.

Q: Which French aviator disappeared in 1944 during a reconnaissance mission over the Mediterranean?
A: Antoine de Saint-Exupéry (repeated in context but different detail).

Q: What happened to the Spanish treasure fleet of 1715, which was lost in a hurricane off the coast of Florida?

A: The fleet sank, and much of the treasure remains undiscovered.

Remarkable Relics and Artifacts

Explore the world of remarkable relics with this trivia section, highlighting intriguing artifacts and their unusual backstories.

From ancient treasures to quirky historical objects, discover the secrets and surprises behind these extraordinary finds. Learn about the significance of each relic, the mysteries they hold, and the often unexpected tales of how they came to be.

This section celebrates the rich history and fascinating narratives encapsulated in some of the world's most extraordinary artifacts.

Q: Which ancient artifact, discovered in 1799, helped scholars decipher Egyptian hieroglyphs?
A: The Rosetta Stone.

Q: What is the name of the prehistoric monument in England composed of a ring of standing stones?
A: Stonehenge.

Q: Which famous Greek statue, known for its missing arms, was discovered on the island of Milos in 1820?
A: Venus de Milo.

Q: What ancient Roman city, buried by the eruption of Mount Vesuvius in 79 AD, was rediscovered in the 18th century?
A: Pompeii.

Q: Which medieval artifact, claimed to be the burial cloth of Jesus, is housed in the Cathedral of Saint John the Baptist in Turin, Italy?
A: The Shroud of Turin.

Q: What ancient stone structure, located in Peru, is believed to have been a royal estate of the Inca emperor Pachacuti?
A: Machu Picchu.

Q: What is the name of the solid gold death mask of the Egyptian Pharaoh Tutankhamun?
A: The Mask of Tutankhamun.

Q: Which ancient manuscript, written in Latin, is a medieval illuminated Christian manuscript containing the four Gospels?
A: The Book of Kells.

Q: What is the name of the collection of ancient texts discovered in a cave near the Dead Sea in the 1940s?
A: The Dead Sea Scrolls.

Q: Which famous British ship, built for King Henry VIII, sank on its maiden voyage in 1545 and was raised in 1982?
A: The Mary Rose.

Q: What is the name of the large, ancient stone calendar created by the Aztecs and discovered in Mexico City?
A: The Aztec Sun Stone.

Q: Which terracotta army, buried with China's first Emperor Qin Shi Huang, was discovered in 1974?
A: The Terracotta Army.

Q: What ancient stone circle in the south of England is believed to have been constructed around 2500 BC?
A: Stonehenge.

Q: Which Viking-age ship, discovered in a burial mound in Norway, is one of the best-preserved Viking ships in the world?
A: The Oseberg Ship.

Q: What ancient Egyptian artifact, a painted limestone bust, depicts the Queen Nefertiti?
A: The Bust of Nefertiti.

Q: Which significant bronze statue of a Greek warrior was recovered from the sea off the coast of Greece in 1972?
A: The Riace Bronzes.

Q: What ancient relic, believed to be a chalice used by Jesus at the Last Supper, is housed in Valencia, Spain?
A: The Holy Grail.

Q: What ancient gold artifact, discovered in 1939 at Sutton Hoo, is believed to be the helmet of an Anglo-Saxon king?
A: The Sutton Hoo Helmet.

Q: Which ancient Greek statue, famous for its depiction of a winged victory, is housed in the Louvre Museum in Paris?
A: The Winged Victory of Samothrace.

Q: What medieval artifact, considered one of the finest examples of Anglo-Saxon art, was discovered in the early 20th century in England?
A: The Alfred Jewel.

Q: Which ancient Roman relic, depicting an emperor on horseback, is one of the few remaining bronze statues from antiquity?
A: The Equestrian Statue of Marcus Aurelius.

Q: What is the name of the prehistoric cave in France, famous for its Paleolithic paintings?
A: Lascaux Cave.

Q: Which ancient Greek sculpture, known for its realistic depiction of the human body, was created by the sculptor Myron?
A: The Discobolus (Discus Thrower).

Q: What significant medieval artifact, a richly decorated book of psalms, was discovered in a peat bog in Ireland?
A: The Faddan More Psalter.

Q: Which ancient relic, believed to be the burial shroud of Jesus, bears the image of a man?
A: The Shroud of Turin.

Q: What is the name of the ancient Roman amphitheater, famous for its gladiatorial games, located in Rome?
A: The Colosseum.

Q: Which ancient Egyptian artifact, a massive stone slab, was key to understanding hieroglyphs?
A: The Rosetta Stone.

Q: What is the name of the ancient structure in Rome that was originally a temple to all the gods and later a Christian church?
A: The Pantheon.

Q: Which medieval artifact, an embroidered cloth nearly 70 meters long, depicts the events leading up to the Norman Conquest of England?
A: The Bayeux Tapestry.

Q: What is the name of the prehistoric monument in Wiltshire, England, consisting of a ring of standing stones?
A: Stonehenge.

Q: Which ancient Greek vase, depicting Achilles and Ajax playing a game, is a famous example of black-figure pottery?
A: The Exekias Vase.

Q: What ancient artifact, found in King Tutankhamun's tomb, is a golden throne with intricate inlays of semiprecious stones?
A: The Golden Throne of Tutankhamun.

Q: Which ancient Roman relic, a stone with inscriptions, was used as a mile marker on the Appian Way?
A: The Milliarium Aureum (Golden Milestone).

Q: What medieval artifact, a manuscript containing the Christian Gospels, was created in the monastery of Iona around 800 AD?
A: The Book of Kells.

Q: Which ancient Greek temple, dedicated to the goddess Athena, stands on the Acropolis in Athens?
A: The Parthenon.

Q: What significant prehistoric artifact, found in Austria, is a small statuette of a female figure believed to represent fertility?
A: The Venus of Willendorf.

Q: Which ancient Egyptian artifact, a stone bust, depicts Queen Nefertiti and is housed in the Neues Museum in Berlin?
A: The Bust of Nefertiti.

Q: What is the name of the ancient city carved into rock in Jordan, famous for its architecture and water conduit system?
A: Petra.

Q: Which ancient Roman sculpture, depicting a she-wolf suckling Romulus and Remus, symbolizes the founding of Rome?
A: The Capitoline Wolf.

Q: What ancient artifact, discovered in a cave in the 1940s, contains the oldest known surviving copies of biblical texts?
A: The Dead Sea Scrolls.

Q: Which ancient Greek statue, discovered in fragments on the island of Samothrace, represents the goddess of victory?
A: The Winged Victory of Samothrace.

Q: What ancient structure in Egypt, originally built as a tomb for Pharaoh Khufu, is one of the Seven Wonders of the Ancient World?
A: The Great Pyramid of Giza.

Q: Which medieval artifact, believed to be the crown worn by Charlemagne, is housed in the Vienna Hofburg?
A: The Imperial Crown of the Holy Roman Empire.

Q: What ancient Roman relic, a triumphal arch, was built to commemorate the victory of Emperor Titus in the Jewish War?
A: The Arch of Titus.

Q: Which ancient Greek sculpture, depicting a young athlete binding his hair, was created by Lysippos?
A: The Apoxyomenos (The Scraper).

Q: What is the name of the ancient Mesoamerican city in Mexico, famous for its large pyramid dedicated to the sun god?
A: Teotihuacan.

Q: Which medieval artifact, a silver reliquary, is believed to contain the bones of Saint James and is housed in Santiago de Compostela?
A: The Reliquary of Saint James.

Q: What ancient Roman artifact, a well-preserved bronze statue, depicts a boy pulling a thorn from his foot?
A: The Spinario (Boy with Thorn).

Q: Which significant prehistoric artifact, discovered in France, is a cave painting of a bison from the Paleolithic era?
A: The Altamira Cave Paintings.

Q: What ancient Egyptian relic, a large stone tablet, was discovered in the tomb of Pharaoh Amenhotep III?
A: The Colossal Statues of Amenhotep III (Memnon Statues).

Q: Which ancient Greek vase, depicting scenes from the Trojan War, is a famous example of red-figure pottery?
A: The Berlin Painter's Amphora.

Q: What is the name of the medieval artifact, a richly decorated book of hours created for Jean, Duke of Berry?
A: The Très Riches Heures du Duc de Berry.

Q: Which ancient Roman artifact, a statue of a general, was discovered in the ruins of the Baths of Caracalla in Rome?
A: The Farnese Hercules.

Q: What significant medieval artifact, an intricately carved ivory chess set, was discovered on the Isle of Lewis in Scotland?
A: The Lewis Chessmen.

Q: Which ancient Egyptian relic, a large obelisk, was transported to Paris and stands in the Place de la Concorde?
A: The Luxor Obelisk.

Q: What is the name of the ancient manuscript, written by Julius Caesar, that details his campaigns in Gaul?
A: Commentarii de Bello Gallico (Commentaries on the Gallic War).

Q: Which ancient Greek sculpture, depicting the goddess Athena, once stood in the Parthenon in Athens?
A: The Athena Parthenos.

Q: What medieval artifact, a beautifully illuminated book, is considered one of the greatest achievements of medieval Irish art?
A: The Book of Kells.

Q: Which ancient Roman relic, a massive stone sarcophagus, was discovered in the tomb of Emperor Septimius Severus?
A: The Sarcophagus of Septimius Severus.

Q: What is the name of the prehistoric artifact, a carved stone circle in Scotland believed to be a ceremonial site?
A: The Callanish Stones.

Q: Which ancient Egyptian relic, a massive temple complex dedicated to the sun god Ra, is located in Thebes?
A: The Temple of Karnak.

Q: What significant medieval artifact, a richly decorated cross, was created by the Anglo-Saxon goldsmith known as "Æthelwulf"?
A: The Alfred Jewel.

Q: Which ancient Greek sculpture, depicting the god Apollo, was discovered on the island of Delos?
A: The Delian Apollo.

Q: What ancient Roman artifact, a triumphal column, was erected to commemorate the victories of Emperor Trajan in the Dacian Wars?
A: Trajan's Column.

Q: Which significant prehistoric artifact, a carved ivory figurine, is one of the oldest known depictions of the human form?
A: The Venus of Hohle Fels.

Q: What is the name of the ancient city in Turkey, famous for its massive stone heads of gods and kings?
A: Mount Nemrut.

Q: Which medieval artifact, a richly decorated manuscript containing the four Gospels, was created in the monastery of Lindisfarne?
A: The Lindisfarne Gospels.

Q: What ancient Greek sculpture, depicting the goddess of victory, was discovered in the sanctuary of the Great Gods on Samothrace?
A: The Winged Victory of Samothrace.

Q: Which ancient Roman relic, a massive aqueduct, was built to supply water to the city of Nîmes in France?
A: The Pont du Gard.

Q: What is the name of the ancient Egyptian artifact, a large stone statue of a sphinx with the head of a pharaoh?
A: The Great Sphinx of Giza.

Q: Which medieval artifact, a beautifully decorated helmet, was discovered in a ship burial at Sutton Hoo?
A: The Sutton Hoo Helmet.

Q: What ancient Greek sculpture, depicting a charioteer, was discovered in the sanctuary of Apollo at Delphi?
A: The Charioteer of Delphi.

Q: Which significant prehistoric artifact, a carved stone circle in Ireland, is believed to be older than Stonehenge?
A: Newgrange.

Q: What ancient Roman relic, a large amphitheater, is one of the best-preserved examples of Roman architecture?
A: The Colosseum.

Q: Which medieval artifact, a richly decorated reliquary, is believed to contain the head of Saint John the Baptist?
A: The Reliquary of Saint John the Baptist.

Q: What is the name of the ancient Greek sculpture, depicting the god Zeus, that once stood in the Temple of Zeus at Olympia?
A: The Statue of Zeus at Olympia.

Q: Which ancient Roman relic, a large stone bridge, was built to span the Gardon River in France?
A: The Pont du Gard.

Q: What significant prehistoric artifact, a carved stone monolith, is located in the valley of the River Boyne in Ireland?
A: The Lia Fáil (Stone of Destiny).

Q: Which ancient Greek sculpture, depicting a lion attacking a horse, was discovered in the Mausoleum at Halicarnassus?
A: The Lion of Knidos.

Q: What is the name of the medieval artifact, a richly decorated chalice, believed to have been used by Jesus at the Last Supper?
A: The Holy Grail.

Q: Which ancient Egyptian relic, a massive stone statue of a pharaoh, was discovered in the ruins of Memphis?
A: The Colossus of Ramses II.

Q: What significant medieval artifact, a beautifully illuminated manuscript, was created by the monks of the Abbey of Saint Gall?
A: The Saint Gall Gospel Book.

Q: Which ancient Greek sculpture, depicting the goddess Aphrodite, was discovered on the island of Melos?
A: The Venus de Milo.

Q: What ancient Roman relic, a large stone theater, is one of the best-preserved examples of Roman architecture in France?
A: The Theatre of Orange.

Q: Which medieval artifact, a richly decorated brooch, was discovered in a hoard in Ireland?
A: The Tara Brooch.

Q: What is the name of the ancient Egyptian artifact, a large stone obelisk, that was transported to Rome and now stands in the Piazza del Popolo?
A: The Flaminian Obelisk.

Q: Which ancient Greek sculpture, depicting a discus thrower, is one of the most famous examples of classical Greek art?
A: The Discobolus.

Q: What significant prehistoric artifact, a carved stone circle in Scotland, is believed to be a ceremonial site?
A: The Ring of Brodgar.

Q: Which ancient Roman relic, a massive stone arch, was built to commemorate the victory of Emperor Constantine in the Battle of Milvian Bridge?
A: The Arch of Constantine.

Q: What is the name of the medieval artifact, a beautifully decorated manuscript, that was created in the monastery of Echternach?
A: The Echternach Gospels.

Q: Which ancient Greek sculpture, depicting a warrior preparing for battle, was discovered on the island of Aegina?
A: The Aegina Warrior.

Q: What ancient Roman relic, a large stone column, was erected to commemorate the victories of Emperor Marcus Aurelius?

A: The Column of Marcus Aurelius.

Q: Which significant prehistoric artifact, a carved stone monolith, is located in the valley of the River Boyne in Ireland?
A: The Lia Fáil (Stone of Destiny).

Q: What is the name of the ancient Greek sculpture, depicting the goddess Athena, that once stood in the Parthenon in Athens?
A: The Athena Parthenos.

Q: Which medieval artifact, a richly decorated manuscript, is considered one of the finest examples of Anglo-Saxon art?
A: The Lindisfarne Gospels.

Q: What ancient Roman relic, a massive stone amphitheater, is one of the best-preserved examples of Roman architecture in France?
A: The Arena of Nîmes.

Q: Which significant prehistoric artifact, a carved stone circle in Ireland, is believed to be older than Stonehenge?
A: Newgrange.

Q: What is the name of the ancient Egyptian artifact, a large stone statue of a sphinx with the head of a pharaoh?
A: The Great Sphinx of Giza.

Q: Which ancient Greek sculpture, depicting a charioteer, was discovered in the sanctuary of Apollo at Delphi?
A: The Charioteer of Delphi.

Unexpected Alliances and Friendships

Dive into the world of unexpected alliances with this trivia section, exploring surprising partnerships that changed the course of history.

Discover how unlikely allies—from rival nations to historical enemies—joined forces for mutual benefit or surprising outcomes. Learn about the motives behind these unexpected collaborations and their significant impacts.

This section highlights the intriguing and often overlooked alliances that reshaped political landscapes, fostered innovation, and led to unexpected triumphs.

Q: Which unlikely duo from ancient Rome, one a famous general and the other a slave gladiator, formed an alliance during the Third Servile War?
A: Spartacus and Crixus.

Q: Which medieval king of England formed a surprising alliance with Saladin during the Third Crusade?
A: Richard the Lionheart.

Q: Which Native American chief formed an unexpected friendship with the Pilgrims, helping them survive their first winter in the New World?
A: Squanto.

Q: Which French military leader formed an alliance with the Ottoman Empire during the 16th century, defying religious and cultural expectations?

A: Francis I of France.

Q: Which American Founding Father forged a surprising friendship with the French diplomat Pierre Beaumarchais, aiding the American Revolution?
A: Benjamin Franklin.

Q: Which Japanese samurai leader formed an unexpected alliance with Portuguese traders in the 16th century, introducing firearms to Japan?
A: Oda Nobunaga.

Q: Which Russian tsar formed a surprising alliance with the German state of Prussia during the Seven Years' War?
A: Peter III of Russia.

Q: Which African king of the Kingdom of Kongo established a surprising friendship with the Portuguese in the 15th century?
A: King Nzinga a Nkuwu.

Q: Which American Civil War general formed an unexpected alliance with the Cherokee leader Stand Watie?
A: Brigadier General Albert Pike.

Q: Which famous British author formed a surprising friendship with an African American civil rights leader, W.E.B. Du Bois, in the early 20th century?
A: H.G. Wells.

Q: Which German Chancellor formed a surprising alliance with socialist labor leader Ferdinand Lassalle in the 19th century?
A: Otto von Bismarck.

Q: Which British Prime Minister formed an unexpected wartime alliance with Soviet leader Joseph Stalin during World War II?
A: Winston Churchill.

Q: Which Persian ruler formed a surprising alliance with the Greek city-state of Sparta during the Peloponnesian War?
A: Artaxerxes II.

Q: Which American president formed an unexpected friendship with Chinese leader Mao Zedong, leading to a historic visit in 1972?
A: Richard Nixon.

Q: Which French revolutionary leader formed a surprising alliance with the Haitian revolutionary Toussaint Louverture?
A: Étienne Polverel.

Q: Which ancient Egyptian pharaoh formed an unexpected friendship with a Hittite king, leading to the first known peace treaty?
A: Ramses II with Hattusili III.

Q: Which British king formed a surprising alliance with the Mughal emperor Jahangir in the early 17th century?
A: King James I.

Q: Which American industrialist formed an unexpected partnership with Soviet leader Joseph Stalin during World War II to provide military supplies?
A: Henry Ford.

Q: Which Roman emperor formed a surprising alliance with the Germanic chieftain Arminius before their infamous betrayal?
A: Augustus with Arminius.

Q: Which American civil rights leader formed an unexpected friendship with Indian independence leader Mahatma Gandhi?
A: Martin Luther King Jr.

Q: Which Viking leader formed a surprising alliance with the Frankish king Charles the Bald?
A: Rollo.

Q: Which British explorer formed an unexpected friendship with the Hawaiian king Kalaniʻōpuʻu?
A: Captain James Cook.

Q: Which Chinese Communist leader formed an unexpected alliance with the American General Joseph Stilwell during World War II?
A: Mao Zedong.

Q: Which medieval English king formed a surprising alliance with the Scottish rebel William Wallace?
A: Robert the Bruce.

Q: Which French Enlightenment philosopher formed an unexpected friendship with the Prussian king Frederick the Great?
A: Voltaire.

Q: Which Mongol leader formed a surprising alliance with the Christian king of Georgia during the 13th century?
A: Hulagu Khan.

Q: Which American frontiersman formed an unexpected friendship with the Shawnee chief Tecumseh?
A: William Henry Harrison.

Q: Which Italian Renaissance artist formed a surprising friendship with the notorious political figure Niccolò Machiavelli?
A: Leonardo da Vinci.

Q: Which Spanish explorer formed an unexpected alliance with the Inca emperor Atahualpa before ultimately betraying him?
A: Francisco Pizarro.

Q: Which British Prime Minister formed an unexpected alliance with the Soviet leader Mikhail Gorbachev during the 1980s?
A: Margaret Thatcher.

Q: Which French emperor formed a surprising alliance with the Ottoman Sultan Selim III in the late 18th century?
A: Napoleon Bonaparte.

Q: Which American Revolutionary War general formed an unexpected friendship with the Polish military engineer Tadeusz Kościuszko?
A: Thomas Jefferson.

Q: Which British naval officer formed an unexpected alliance with the Maori chief Hongi Hika in the early 19th century?
A: Thomas Kendall.

Q: Which ancient Greek philosopher formed a surprising friendship with the Persian king Cyrus the Younger?
A: Xenophon.

Q: Which American abolitionist formed an unexpected friendship with the British author Charles Dickens?
A: Frederick Douglass.

Q: Which Japanese shogun formed a surprising alliance with the Dutch during the 17th century, despite Japan's isolationist policies?
A: Tokugawa Ieyasu.

Q: Which Roman general formed an unexpected alliance with the Egyptian queen Cleopatra?
A: Julius Caesar.

Q: Which American inventor formed a surprising friendship with the Serbian scientist Nikola Tesla?
A: Thomas Edison.

Q: Which medieval queen of France formed an unexpected alliance with the English king Henry II during the 12th century?
A: Eleanor of Aquitaine.

Q: Which Russian czar formed a surprising alliance with the French military leader Napoleon Bonaparte in 1807?
A: Alexander I.

Q: Which American president formed an unexpected friendship with the Soviet premier Nikita Khrushchev during the 1950s?
A: Dwight D. Eisenhower.

Q: Which African king formed a surprising alliance with the British explorer David Livingstone in the 19th century?
A: King Mutesa I of Buganda.

Q: Which Spanish queen formed an unexpected alliance with the Moorish king of Granada, Boabdil, during the Reconquista?
A: Isabella I of Castile.

Q: Which American Civil War general formed a surprising friendship with the Sioux chief Red Cloud?
A: General George Crook.

Q: Which ancient Greek king formed an unexpected alliance with the Persian king Darius III?
A: Alexander the Great (briefly before turning against him).

Q: Which British archaeologist formed an unexpected friendship with the Bedouin leader Sheikh Hamoudi?
A: T.E. Lawrence (Lawrence of Arabia).

Q: Which French king formed a surprising alliance with the Ottoman Sultan Suleiman the Magnificent?
A: Francis I of France.

Q: Which American cowboy formed an unexpected friendship with the English author Sir Arthur Conan Doyle?
A: Buffalo Bill Cody.

Q: Which Indian leader formed a surprising alliance with the British during the Indian Rebellion of 1857?
A: Maharaja Gulab Singh.

Q: Which ancient Chinese general formed an unexpected alliance with the Xiongnu chieftain Modu Chanyu?
A: General Huo Qubing.

Q: Which Italian revolutionary formed a surprising friendship with the British prime minister William Gladstone?
A: Giuseppe Garibaldi.

Q: Which French revolutionary leader formed an unexpected alliance with the Haitian revolutionary Jean-Jacques Dessalines?
A: General Charles Leclerc.

Q: Which American president formed an unexpected friendship with the Japanese emperor Hirohito after World War II?
A: Harry S. Truman.

Q: Which British explorer formed a surprising alliance with the Ashanti king Prempeh I in the 19th century?
A: Sir Francis Scott.

Q: Which ancient Roman general formed an unexpected friendship with the Parthian king Orodes II?
A: Mark Antony.

Q: Which American civil rights leader formed an unexpected alliance with the Indian Prime Minister Jawaharlal Nehru?
A: Martin Luther King Jr.

Q: Which medieval Scottish king formed a surprising alliance with the Norwegian king Haakon IV?
A: Alexander III of Scotland.

Q: Which Russian revolutionary leader formed an unexpected alliance with the German emperor Wilhelm II during World War I?
A: Vladimir Lenin.

Q: Which French author formed a surprising friendship with the British prime minister Benjamin Disraeli?
A: Victor Hugo.

Q: Which American cowboy formed an unexpected friendship with the Sioux chief Sitting Bull?
A: Buffalo Bill Cody.

Q: Which Italian politician formed a surprising alliance with the Ethiopian emperor Haile Selassie during World War II?
A: Benito Mussolini.

Q: Which American president formed an unexpected friendship with the Soviet premier Leonid Brezhnev in the 1970s?
A: Richard Nixon.

Q: Which British explorer formed a surprising alliance with the Maori chief Te Pahi in the early 19th century?
A: Samuel Marsden.

Q: Which ancient Egyptian queen formed an unexpected alliance with the Roman general Mark Antony?
A: Cleopatra VII.

Q: Which American industrialist formed a surprising friendship with the German chancellor Otto von Bismarck in the 19th century?
A: Andrew Carnegie.

Fantastic Feasts and Holiday Fests

Indulge in the world of fantastic feasts with this trivia section, featuring extravagant banquets and unusual foods from history.

Explore opulent celebrations where the menu was as grand as the occasion, including bizarre and exotic dishes served to impress guests. Discover the stories behind these lavish events, the eccentricities of the hosts, and the culinary curiosities that defined these memorable gatherings.

This section offers a delectable glimpse into the art of extravagant dining through the ages.

Q: Which ancient Roman festival, celebrated on December 17, involved role reversals between masters and slaves?
A: Saturnalia.

Q: During which medieval European feast would participants throw beans to select a "King of the Bean"?
A: Twelfth Night.

Q: Which ancient Persian festival, still celebrated today, marks the Persian New Year with a feast including dishes like Sabzi Polo Mahi (herbed rice with fish)?
A: Nowruz.

Q: Which ancient Greek festival, held every four years in Olympia, featured both athletic contests and grand feasts?

A: The Olympic Games.

Q: Which Chinese festival involves feasting on mooncakes and celebrates the harvest and the full moon?
A: Mid-Autumn Festival.

Q: Which Jewish holiday, celebrated with a Seder meal, commemorates the Exodus from Egypt?
A: Passover.

Q: Which Indian festival of lights involves feasting on sweets and savory dishes and marks the victory of light over darkness?
A: Diwali.

Q: During which medieval French festival would a "Lord of Misrule" lead revelry and feasting?
A: Feast of Fools.

Q: Which British holiday, known for its grand feast with turkey and pudding, celebrates the birth of Jesus Christ?
A: Christmas.

Q: Which ancient Egyptian festival, celebrated with feasting and drinking, honored the goddess Hathor?
A: Festival of Drunkenness.

Q: Which Spanish festival features a feast with seafood paella and is celebrated on the day of St. James?
A: La Fiesta de Santiago.

Q: Which Japanese holiday involves feasting on special dishes like osechi-ryōri and marks the beginning of the new year?

A: Oshogatsu (New Year).

Q: Which Mexican holiday involves a feast with tamales and honors the deceased?
A: Day of the Dead (Día de los Muertos).

Q: During which ancient Mesopotamian festival did people feast and celebrate the god Marduk's victory over Tiamat?
A: Akitu Festival.

Q: Which modern American holiday involves a feast with turkey, stuffing, and pie, celebrating the Pilgrims' harvest?
A: Thanksgiving.

Q: Which Scottish festival, celebrated with haggis and whisky, marks the life of the poet Robert Burns?
A: Burns Night.

Q: Which Brazilian festival, known for its parades and samba, includes feasting before Lent?
A: Carnival.

Q: Which South Korean harvest festival involves feasting on songpyeon (rice cakes) and honoring ancestors?
A: Chuseok.

Q: During which Islamic holiday do Muslims break their fast with a feast known as Iftar?
A: Ramadan.

Q: Which German festival, originally a royal wedding celebration, is now known for its beer and pretzels?

A: Oktoberfest.

Q: Which French holiday, celebrated with galette des rois, marks the visit of the Magi to the baby Jesus?
A: Epiphany.

Q: Which ancient Roman feast involved consuming copious amounts of food and drink in honor of Bacchus, the god of wine?
A: Bacchanalia.

Q: Which Caribbean festival, featuring a feast with jerk chicken and plantains, celebrates emancipation from slavery?
A: Emancipation Day.

Q: Which West African festival involves a feast with jollof rice and celebrates the end of the harvest season?
A: Yam Festival.

Q: Which Jewish holiday involves feasting on dairy foods like cheesecake and commemorates the giving of the Torah at Mount Sinai?
A: Shavuot.

Q: During which ancient Celtic festival, celebrated with feasting and bonfires, do people mark the end of the harvest season and the beginning of winter?
A: Samhain.

Q: Which Italian holiday involves a feast with seven types of seafood and celebrates Christmas Eve?
A: Feast of the Seven Fishes.

Q: Which Hindu festival, marked by feasting and colorful powders, celebrates the arrival of spring and the victory of good over evil?
A: Holi.

Q: Which Swedish holiday involves a feast with pickled herring and schnapps and celebrates the longest day of the year?
A: Midsummer.

Q: Which ancient Greek festival, involving a feast with lamb and barley, honored the goddess Demeter?
A: Thesmophoria.

Q: Which Roman Catholic feast, celebrated with a grand meal and special pastries, honors the Virgin Mary on August 15th?
A: Assumption of Mary.

Q: Which traditional Japanese festival involves feasting on eels and celebrates the dead during the summer?
A: Obon.

Q: Which South American festival, featuring a feast with grilled meats, celebrates the national day of Argentina?
A: Día de la Revolución de Mayo.

Q: Which ancient Norse festival involved feasting and drinking to honor the gods and celebrate the winter solstice?
A: Yule.

Q: Which American holiday, celebrated with barbecues and fireworks, marks the independence of the United States?
A: Fourth of July (Independence Day).

Q: Which Filipino festival involves a feast with lechon (roast pig) and celebrates the feast of the Santo Niño?
A: Sinulog.

Q: Which ancient Chinese festival involves a feast with sticky rice dumplings and commemorates the poet Qu Yuan?
A: Dragon Boat Festival.

Q: Which Irish holiday involves feasting on corned beef and cabbage and celebrates the patron saint of Ireland?
A: St. Patrick's Day.

Q: Which Russian holiday, celebrated with a feast of blini (pancakes), marks the end of winter and the beginning of Lent?
A: Maslenitsa.

Q: Which French-Canadian holiday, celebrated with a feast of tourtière (meat pie), marks the end of the year?
A: Réveillon.

Q: Which Spanish festival, known for its tomato fight, involves a pre-fight feast and celebrates the end of summer?
A: La Tomatina.

Q: Which Turkish holiday involves feasting on sweets like baklava and celebrates the end of Ramadan?
A: Eid al-Fitr.

Q: Which ancient Indian festival involved a grand feast and celebrated the return of King Rama from exile?
A: Diwali.

Q: Which German holiday involves a feast with carp and marks the New Year?
A: Silvester.

Q: Which Dutch holiday, celebrated with a feast of oliebollen (fried dough balls), marks the New Year?
A: New Year's Eve (Oud en Nieuw).

Q: Which ancient Roman holiday, celebrated with feasting and gift-giving, honored the goddess Juno?
A: Matronalia.

Q: Which Brazilian holiday, celebrated with feijoada (black bean stew), marks the independence of Brazil?
A: Independence Day (Sete de Setembro).

Q: Which French festival, featuring a feast with cheese and wine, celebrates the harvest season?
A: Vendanges (Grape Harvest Festival).

Q: Which ancient Egyptian festival, celebrated with a feast and a procession, honored the god Osiris?
A: Festival of Osiris.

Q: Which Ethiopian holiday, marked by a feast with injera (flatbread) and doro wat (chicken stew), celebrates the finding of the True Cross?
A: Meskel.

Q: Which British holiday, involving a feast with roast beef and Yorkshire pudding, celebrates the patron saint of England?
A: St. George's Day.

Q: Which modern holiday, celebrated with a feast of plant-based dishes, honors the planet and promotes environmental awareness?
A: Earth Day.

Q: Which ancient Roman feast, celebrated on February 15th with rituals and feasting, honored the god Lupercus?
A: Lupercalia.

Q: Which Chinese holiday, involving a feast with hot pot and family reunions, marks the end of the lunar new year celebrations?
A: Lantern Festival.

Q: Which Jewish holiday involves feasting on fried foods like latkes and celebrates the rededication of the Holy Temple in Jerusalem?
A: Hanukkah.

Q: Which Spanish holiday, involving a feast with seafood and tapas, celebrates the arrival of the Magi?
A: Three Kings' Day (Día de los Reyes).

Q: Which Irish holiday involves a feast with seafood and celebrates the summer solstice?
A: Lughnasadh.

Q: Which Hindu festival involves a feast with various sweets and celebrates the birth of Krishna?
A: Janmashtami.

Q: Which ancient Greek festival, involving a feast with grapes and wine, honored the god Dionysus?
A: Dionysia.

Eerie and Spooky Events

Delve into the realm of eerie events with this trivia section, uncovering spooky happenings and unexplained phenomena from history.

Explore chilling tales of ghostly apparitions, mysterious occurrences, and supernatural encounters that have intrigued and unsettled people throughout the ages. Discover the legends, investigations, and cultural impacts surrounding these eerie events.

This section provides a spine-tingling look at the unsettling mysteries and haunting stories that continue to captivate and fascinate.

Q: What infamous prison in San Francisco Bay is rumored to be haunted by the ghosts of former inmates?
A: Alcatraz.

Q: Which English queen is said to haunt the Tower of London, where she was executed in 1536?
A: Anne Boleyn.

Q: In which American city did the infamous Salem witch trials take place in 1692?
A: Salem, Massachusetts.

Q: What is the name of the ghost ship that is said to sail the seas, never able to make port?
A: The Flying Dutchman.

Q: Which cursed artifact, said to cause death and disaster, was discovered in the tomb of Tutankhamun?
A: The Curse of the Pharaohs.

Q: Which European city is home to the catacombs that house the skeletal remains of over six million people?
A: Paris, France.

Q: What is the name of the haunted mansion in San Jose, California, built by the widow of the rifle inventor?
A: The Winchester Mystery House.

Q: Which Scottish castle is said to be haunted by the ghost of a drummer boy?
A: Edinburgh Castle.

Q: What unexplained event in 1908 caused a massive explosion in the Siberian wilderness, flattening 2,000 square kilometers of forest?
A: The Tunguska Event.

Q: Which ghostly ship appeared to Prince George of Wales and his brother Albert Victor in 1881?
A: The Phantom Ship of the Flying Dutchman.

Q: In which American city is the LaLaurie Mansion, known for its gruesome history and hauntings, located?
A: New Orleans, Louisiana.

Q: What mysterious disappearance involved a lighthouse keeper and two assistants in 1900 at the Flannan Isles Lighthouse?
A: The Flannan Isles Mystery.

Q: Which American Civil War battlefield is known for its ghost sightings, including soldiers and phantom battles?
A: Gettysburg.

Q: What is the name of the infamous New England inn known for its association with Lizzie Borden and paranormal activity?
A: The Lizzie Borden House.

Q: Which ancient city was buried by the eruption of Mount Vesuvius in 79 AD and is said to be haunted by its victims?
A: Pompeii.

Q: What mysterious occurrence involved nine Russian hikers who died under unexplained circumstances in 1959?
A: The Dyatlov Pass Incident.

Q: Which haunted castle in Romania is associated with the legend of Dracula?
A: Bran Castle.

Q: What eerie phenomenon involves people hearing mysterious, unexplained noises in the sky, known as "The Hum"?
A: Skyquakes.

Q: Which Queen Mary ocean liner is known for its haunted history and ghostly sightings?
A: RMS Queen Mary.

Q: What is the name of the forest in Romania known as one of the most haunted places on Earth?
A: Hoia Baciu Forest.

Q: What eerie natural phenomenon in Norway is believed to be caused by reflections of the sun on the Arctic Circle?
A: The Hessdalen Lights.

Q: Which London site is famously haunted by the ghost of the "Black Dog"?
A: Newgate Prison.

Q: What is the name of the haunted plantation in Louisiana known for its ghost stories and paranormal activity?
A: The Myrtles Plantation.

Q: Which Spanish monastery is known for its sightings of ghostly monks and mysterious voices?
A: Monastery of San Lorenzo de El Escorial.

Q: What is the name of the infamous German castle rumored to be haunted by the ghost of a white lady?
A: Hohenzollern Castle.

Q: Which island off the coast of Mexico is known for its eerie display of hundreds of dolls hanging from trees?
A: Island of the Dolls (Isla de las Muñecas).

Q: What spooky occurrence involved a mysterious figure knocking on doors and windows in rural villages in England in the 19th century?
A: Spring-heeled Jack.

Q: Which historic hotel in Colorado inspired Stephen King's "The Shining" and is reputedly haunted?
A: The Stanley Hotel.

Q: What mysterious disappearance in 1872 involved a ship found adrift with its crew missing?
A: The Mary Celeste.

Q: Which Japanese village is known for its annual tradition of making life-sized dolls to replace deceased residents?
A: Nagoro.

Q: Which cursed diamond, known for bringing misfortune to its owners, is on display at the Smithsonian Institution?
A: The Hope Diamond.

Q: What unexplained event in 1977 involved mysterious sounds from outer space detected by the Big Ear radio telescope?
A: The Wow! Signal.

Q: Which ancient Roman town is rumored to be haunted by the spirits of those who perished in the eruption of Mount Vesuvius?
A: Herculaneum.

Q: What spooky phenomenon involves a ship's light mysteriously appearing off the coast of Maine?
A: The Seguin Island Lighthouse Ghost.

Q: Which abandoned asylum in West Virginia is notorious for its hauntings and ghost tours?
A: Trans-Allegheny Lunatic Asylum.

Q: What ancient English stone circle is rumored to be haunted by ghosts of the people who built it?
A: Stonehenge.

Q: Which American ghost town, abandoned after a mining disaster, is known for its ghostly apparitions?
A: Bodie, California.

Q: What eerie mystery involves ghostly voices recorded on audio equipment, known as EVP?
A: Electronic Voice Phenomena.

Q: Which haunted Irish castle is known for its sightings of a mysterious "Lady in Red"?
A: Leap Castle.

Q: Which American island prison is rumored to be haunted by the ghost of Al Capone?
A: Alcatraz Island.

Q: What unexplained event in the 17th century involved a ship found drifting with its crew dead, appearing to have been frozen to death?
A: The Ghost Ship Octavius.

Q: Which haunted Scottish battlefield is known for ghostly soldiers and eerie sounds of battle?
A: Culloden.

Q: Which famous Italian opera house is said to be haunted by the ghost of a singer who died there?
A: La Fenice in Venice.

Q: What spooky occurrence involves mysterious lights appearing in the skies over Marfa, Texas?
A: The Marfa Lights.

Q: Which English pub, built in the 12th century, is known for its ghostly apparitions and paranormal activity?
A: The Skirrid Mountain Inn.

Q: What eerie discovery was made in the Siberian tundra, consisting of a massive, unexplained crater?
A: The Patomskiy Crater.

Q: Which haunted mansion in Savannah, Georgia, is known for its ghostly residents and eerie occurrences?
A: The Sorrel-Weed House.

Q: What spooky natural phenomenon in Australia involves a glowing light that follows travelers?
A: The Min Min Light.

Q: Which haunted English manor is known for the ghost of a young girl who appears in a blue dress?
A: Borley Rectory.

Q: What eerie event in 1943 involved a ship supposedly becoming invisible and teleporting, known as the "Philadelphia Experiment"?
A: The USS Eldridge Incident.

Q: Which haunted Japanese castle is known for sightings of the ghost of a samurai?
A: Himeji Castle.

Q: What spooky occurrence in the 16th century involved mysterious disappearances on an island in North Carolina?
A: The Lost Colony of Roanoke.

Q: Which Scottish island is rumored to be haunted by the spirits of plague victims who were quarantined there?
A: Inchkeith Island.

Q: What eerie natural phenomenon in Canada involves ghostly apparitions of people and animals on the shores of Lake Superior?
A: The Phantom Ship of Lake Superior.

Q: Which haunted mansion in San Francisco is known for its ghostly inhabitants and eerie occurrences?
A: The Haas-Lilienthal House.

Q: What spooky phenomenon involves mysterious, ghostly lights appearing in the Brown Mountain area of North Carolina?
A: The Brown Mountain Lights.

Q: Which English village is said to be haunted by the ghost of a monk who was executed for witchcraft?
A: Pluckley.

Q: Which haunted Italian island is known for its dark history and ghostly inhabitants?
A: Poveglia Island.

Q: What eerie event in 1962 involved a whole town in Pennsylvania being evacuated due to an underground coal fire?
A: The Centralia Mine Fire.

Q: Which haunted castle in England is known for the ghost of a headless horseman?
A: Chillingham Castle.

Q: What mysterious event in 1973 involved a plane disappearing without a trace in the Bermuda Triangle?
A: The Disappearance of Flight 19.

Q: Which ancient Chinese city is rumored to be haunted by the spirits of those who died building it?
A: Xi'an, home of the Terracotta Army.

Q: What spooky phenomenon involves mysterious, ghostly lights in the skies over Hessdalen, Norway?
A: The Hessdalen Lights.

Q: Which haunted American plantation is known for the ghost of a slave who appears in photos?
A: Myrtles Plantation.

Q: What eerie occurrence in 1987 involved a mysterious "black figure" appearing on a security camera in a London Underground station?
A: The Ghost of Covent Garden Station.

Strange and Uncanny Traditions

Explore the world of strange traditions with this trivia section, showcasing unusual customs and rituals from diverse cultures.

Delve into quirky practices, from unique celebrations to bizarre ceremonies, and discover the meanings and histories behind these fascinating traditions. Learn about the cultural significance, unusual rules, and surprising origins of these customs.

This section offers an intriguing glimpse into the rich tapestry of human behavior and the diverse ways people celebrate and honor their heritage.

Q: Which Spanish festival involves participants throwing tomatoes at each other in a massive food fight?
A: La Tomatina.

Q: In which country do people celebrate New Year's Eve by smashing plates against the doors of friends and family?
A: Denmark.

Q: What is the name of the Thai festival where people release lanterns into the sky to symbolize letting go of misfortunes?
A: Yi Peng.

Q: Which Japanese tradition involves sumo wrestlers trying to make babies cry for good luck?
A: Nakizumo.

Q: In which country do people celebrate Christmas by hiding brooms so that witches can't steal them?
A: Norway.

Q: What is the unusual New Year's Eve tradition in Spain involving eating 12 grapes at midnight?
A: Twelve Grapes of Luck.

Q: Which festival in India celebrates the arrival of spring with a colorful powder-throwing celebration?
A: Holi.

Q: In which country do people celebrate the Festival of the Dead by picnicking in cemeteries?
A: Madagascar.

Q: What unique festival in Thailand features people dressing up as spirits and performing rituals to appease ghosts?
A: Phi Ta Khon.

Q: Which tradition in Finland involves sitting in a hot sauna and then jumping into an icy lake?
A: Ice Swimming.

Q: In which country do people celebrate Easter by dressing up as witches and knocking on doors for treats?
A: Sweden.

Q: What is the name of the Mexican holiday where people build altars and honor deceased loved ones?
A: Día de los Muertos (Day of the Dead).

Q: Which country has a tradition of throwing cinnamon on single people when they turn 25?
A: Denmark.

Q: In which country do people celebrate New Year by throwing furniture out of their windows?
A: South Africa.

Q: What unique Japanese tradition involves making mochi (rice cakes) with large wooden mallets?
A: Mochitsuki.

Q: Which unusual festival in England involves chasing a large wheel of cheese down a steep hill?
A: Cooper's Hill Cheese-Rolling and Wake.

Q: In which country do people wear red underwear on New Year's Eve for good luck?
A: Italy.

Q: What is the name of the Spanish festival where people build massive papier-mâché figures and then burn them?
A: Las Fallas.

Q: In which country do people celebrate a unique Christmas tradition of roller-skating to church?
A: Venezuela.

Q: What unusual tradition in Papua New Guinea involves wearing elaborate wigs made from human hair?
A: Huli Wigmen.

Q: Which country celebrates a holiday called "National Sleepyhead Day" where the last person to wake up is thrown into a lake or the sea?
A: Finland.

Q: In which country do people celebrate weddings with a traditional dance where the bride and groom are lifted on chairs?
A: Israel (Horah dance).

Q: What unusual festival in the United States involves racing outhouses on wheels?
A: Outhouse Races in Michigan.

Q: In which country do people celebrate Midsummer by dancing around a pole and singing frog songs?
A: Sweden.

Q: What is the name of the unique New Year's tradition in Ecuador where people burn effigies to rid themselves of bad luck?
A: Año Viejo.

Q: Which country celebrates a festival called "Ivrea Battle of the Oranges" where participants throw oranges at each other?
A: Italy.

Q: In which country do people hang bread from their doors to ward off evil spirits?
A: Ireland.

Q: What unique Christmas tradition in Japan involves eating KFC for dinner?
A: KFC Christmas Dinner.

Q: Which country has a tradition called "Lopburi Monkey Buffet Festival" where monkeys are treated to a feast?
A: Thailand.

Q: In which country do people celebrate a tradition called "Obon" by floating lanterns on water to honor ancestors?
A: Japan.

Q: What unusual tradition in Spain involves jumping over newborn babies to cleanse them of original sin?
A: El Colacho.

Q: Which country celebrates a festival called "Jarramplas" where participants pelt a man dressed as a devil with turnips?
A: Spain.

Q: In which country do people celebrate a unique tradition of throwing water at each other during their New Year festival?
A: Thailand (Songkran).

Q: What is the name of the Scottish tradition where people first-foot (visit) homes after midnight on New Year's Eve for good luck?
A: Hogmanay.

Q: Which country has a tradition called "Krampusnacht" where a demon-like creature punishes naughty children?
A: Austria.

Q: In which country do people celebrate Christmas by decorating spider webs?
A: Ukraine.

Q: What unusual festival in Japan involves men wearing nothing but loincloths in freezing weather to receive blessings?
A: Hadaka Matsuri.

Q: Which country has a tradition called "Cap Go Meh" where people pierce their cheeks with sharp objects during the Lantern Festival?
A: Indonesia.

Q: In which country do people celebrate a tradition called "La Mordida" where the birthday person's face is pushed into the cake?
A: Mexico.

Q: What unique festival in Scotland involves rolling burning barrels of tar through the streets on New Year's Eve?
A: The Stonehaven Fireballs Ceremony.

Q: Which country has a tradition called "Somba Ke" where people celebrate the winter solstice by dancing around a giant bonfire?
A: Canada (Yellowknife).

Q: In which country do people celebrate a tradition called "Rapa das Bestas" where wild horses are rounded up and their manes are cut?
A: Spain.

Q: What unusual festival in England involves people running through the streets carrying flaming tar barrels?
A: Ottery St. Mary Tar Barrel Festival.

Q: Which country has a tradition called "Puck Fair" where a wild goat is crowned king for three days?
A: Ireland.

Q: In which country do people celebrate a festival called "La Pourcailhade" where pig-themed competitions take place?
A: France.

Q: What is the name of the unique Indian festival where people gather to hurl colored powders at each other?
A: Holi.

Q: Which country celebrates a tradition called "Radish Night" where radishes are carved into intricate designs?
A: Mexico (Noche de Rábanos).

Q: In which country do people celebrate a tradition called "Loy Krathong" by floating baskets decorated with flowers and candles on water?
A: Thailand.

Q: What unusual tradition in Switzerland involves children dressing up as old women and making noise to chase away winter spirits?
A: Chalandamarz.

Q: Which country has a tradition called "Dongzhi" where people eat rice balls called "tangyuan" to celebrate the winter solstice?
A: China.

Q: In which country do people celebrate a tradition called "Nyepi" by remaining silent and shutting down all activities for a day?
A: Indonesia (Bali).

Q: What unique festival in Italy involves people wearing elaborate masks and costumes during a grand carnival?
A: Venice Carnival.

Q: Which country has a tradition called "Jólabókaflóð" where books are exchanged on Christmas Eve and read late into the night?
A: Iceland.

Q: In which country do people celebrate a tradition called "Haro Wine Festival" by having a massive wine fight?
A: Spain.

Q: What unusual tradition in Germany involves hiding a pickle ornament in the Christmas tree for good luck?
A: The Christmas Pickle.

Q: Which country celebrates a festival called "Up Helly Aa" where a Viking ship is burned to mark the end of Yule?
A: Scotland (Shetland Islands).

Q: In which country do people celebrate a tradition called "Gion Matsuri" by parading massive floats through the streets?
A: Japan.

Q: What unique festival in the Philippines involves dressing up in giant masks and costumes made of papier-mâché?
A: The Giant Lantern Festival.

Q: Which country has a tradition called "Songkran" where people engage in massive water fights to celebrate the New Year?
A: Thailand.

Q: In which country do people celebrate a tradition called "San Fermín" by running with the bulls through the streets?
A: Spain.

Q: What unusual festival in India involves people walking on hot coals to prove their devotion?
A: Theemithi.

Q: Which country celebrates a tradition called "Kukeri" where people dress in elaborate costumes to scare away evil spirits?
A: Bulgaria.

Q: In which country do people celebrate a tradition called "Burning Man" by building and burning large wooden effigies?
A: United States.

Q: What unique festival in Finland involves racing with a partner slung over your shoulder?
A: Wife Carrying Championship.

Q: Which country has a tradition called "Maslenitsa" where people celebrate the end of winter by eating pancakes and burning a straw effigy?
A: Russia.

Uncommon Crimes and Heists

Uncover the world of uncommon crimes with this trivia section, highlighting outlandish heists, bizarre scams, and peculiar criminal acts.

Discover the creative and sometimes absurd methods used by criminals to carry out their schemes, and learn about the unusual motives and remarkable outcomes of these notorious cases.

From elaborate cons to quirky criminal enterprises, this section offers a captivating look at the imaginative and often surprising side of crime throughout history.

Q: What notorious heist in 1976 saw thieves digging a tunnel to rob a bank in Nice, France?
A: The Société Générale Bank Heist.

Q: Which unsolved art heist in 1990 involved the theft of 13 pieces of art worth $500 million from a museum in Boston?
A: The Isabella Stewart Gardner Museum Heist.

Q: What unusual theft in 2004 involved the heist of Edvard Munch's famous painting "The Scream" in Oslo?
A: The Munch Museum Heist.

Q: Which famous heist in 1963 involved the robbery of £2.6 million from a Royal Mail train in England?
A: The Great Train Robbery.

Q: What peculiar 2006 crime involved the theft of a 10-ton bridge in the Czech Republic?
A: The Velka Chuchle Bridge Heist.

Q: Which 1971 crime involved a man hijacking a plane, collecting a ransom, and then parachuting out, never to be seen again?
A: The D.B. Cooper Hijacking.

Q: What 2008 heist in Ireland involved thieves stealing €7.6 million from a bank by kidnapping the manager's family?
A: The Bank of Ireland Heist.

Q: Which bizarre 1995 robbery involved the theft of a truckload of Bull semen in California?
A: The Bull Semen Heist. While the theft of bull semen sounds gross and odd, semen from a prized bull may in fact be highly valuable for breeding purposes.

Q: What unusual crime in 1983 saw thieves stealing £26 million worth of gold bullion from a warehouse near Heathrow Airport?
A: The Brink's-Mat Robbery.

Q: Which notorious heist in 2000 saw thieves making off with $55 million in diamonds from a Belgian bank?
A: The Antwerp Diamond Heist.

Q: What quirky 2012 crime involved the theft of 6,000 liters of maple syrup in Canada?
A: The Great Canadian Maple Syrup Heist.

Q: Which heist in 1994 involved thieves stealing $17.3 million from an armored car depot in the U.S.?

A: The Dunbar Armored Robbery.

Q: What unusual crime in 2005 saw thieves stealing an entire church in Russia brick by brick?
A: The Missing Church Heist.

Q: Which notorious heist in 2003 involved the theft of $70 million worth of jewelry from a vault in Belgium?
A: The Antwerp Diamond Center Heist.

Q: What 2013 theft in Germany involved the heist of a 220-pound solid gold coin from a museum?
A: The Big Maple Leaf Heist.

Q: Which unusual crime in 2007 involved thieves stealing 12 million Yen from a moving vehicle in Japan?
A: The Hiroshima Armored Car Heist.

Q: What 1997 robbery involved a group of thieves stealing $18.9 million from the Loomis Fargo vault in North Carolina?
A: The Loomis Fargo Heist.

Q: Which peculiar theft in 2012 involved the heist of an 800-pound bronze statue from a cemetery in Norway?
A: The Stolen Statue of Emanuel Vigeland.

Q: What unusual 2010 crime involved the theft of a 2,400-year-old sarcophagus from a museum in Egypt?
A: The Egyptian Sarcophagus Heist.

Q: Which bizarre 2004 theft involved the heist of 2,000 gallons of liquid nitrogen from a lab in California?

A: The Liquid Nitrogen Heist.

Q: What unusual heist in 1980 saw thieves stealing 17 tons of silver bars from a warehouse in Canada?
A: The Montreal Silver Heist.

Q: Which 2015 crime involved the theft of a $150,000 violin from a train in Germany?
A: The Stolen Stradivarius.

Q: What 2003 robbery involved the theft of $39 million worth of gold and cash from a bank in Brazil?
A: The Banco Central Heist.

Q: Which quirky 2009 theft involved the heist of a 1,500-pound church bell from a monastery in Greece?
A: The Stolen Church Bell Heist.

Q: What unusual 2001 crime involved the theft of 300 tons of steel beams from a construction site in the U.S.?
A: The Steel Beam Heist.

Q: Which notorious heist in 1978 involved the robbery of $5 million from Lufthansa cargo at JFK Airport?
A: The Lufthansa Heist.

Q: What bizarre 2014 theft involved the heist of 9 million bees from a beekeeper in Italy?
A: The Bee Heist.

Q: Which unusual crime in 2016 involved the theft of 100 rare books from a library in London?

A: The Stolen Books Heist.

Q: What 2000 robbery involved the theft of $240 million worth of diamonds from a jewelry store in Amsterdam?
A: The Schiphol Airport Heist.

Q: Which quirky 2011 theft involved the heist of 3,000 pairs of designer shoes from a warehouse in France?
A: The Shoe Heist.

Q: What unusual 1985 crime involved the theft of 13 tons of gold bullion from a vault in Brazil?
A: The Rio de Janeiro Gold Heist.

Q: Which bizarre 2013 robbery involved thieves stealing 200,000 liters of red wine from a vineyard in France?
A: The Wine Heist.

Q: What notorious 2002 crime involved the theft of $1 billion worth of artifacts from a museum in Baghdad?
A: The Iraqi National Museum Heist.

Q: Which unusual 2008 theft involved the heist of 2 million chocolate eggs from a warehouse in the U.K.?
A: The Chocolate Egg Heist.

Q: What quirky 2007 robbery involved the theft of a 40-ton tanker full of olive oil in Spain?
A: The Olive Oil Heist.

Q: Which notorious heist in 1984 involved the robbery of $33 million worth of gold from a warehouse in England?

A: The Brinks-Mat Heist.

Q: What unusual 2015 theft involved the heist of 20,000 pounds of cheese from a dairy in Wisconsin?
A: The Cheese Heist.

Q: Which 2012 robbery involved the theft of $120 million worth of jewels from a Cannes hotel?
A: The Cannes Jewel Heist.

Q: What quirky 2009 crime involved the theft of a 6-foot tall inflatable gorilla from a car dealership in California?
A: The Inflatable Gorilla Heist.

Q: Which notorious heist in 1992 involved the robbery of $70 million worth of gold and jewelry from a warehouse in Italy?
A: The Knightsbridge Security Deposit Heist.

Q: What unusual 2000 theft involved the heist of 200 tons of garlic from a farm in China?
A: The Garlic Heist.

Q: Which bizarre 2016 robbery involved the theft of a 1,000-year-old Buddha statue from a temple in Japan?
A: The Buddha Heist.

Q: What 2013 heist involved the theft of $50 million worth of diamonds from a plane in Belgium?
A: The Brussels Airport Diamond Heist.

Q: Which quirky 2004 crime involved the theft of a 20-foot tall rubber duck from a festival in Australia?

A: The Rubber Duck Heist.

Q: What unusual 2011 robbery involved the theft of $100,000 worth of toilet paper from a warehouse in Germany?
A: The Toilet Paper Heist.

Q: Which notorious heist in 1983 involved the robbery of $30 million worth of gold and cash from a warehouse in the U.K.?
A: The Heathrow Airport Gold Heist.

Q: What quirky 2015 theft involved the heist of 200,000 bees from a hive in the U.K.?
A: The Bee Heist.

Q: Which unusual 2014 robbery involved the theft of a 500-pound bronze statue from a park in Brazil?
A: The Bronze Statue Heist.

Q: What notorious 2009 heist involved the robbery of $65 million worth of jewels from a store in London?
A: The Graff Diamonds Heist.

Q: Which quirky 2006 crime involved the theft of a 10-foot tall inflatable Santa from a front yard in the U.S.?
A: The Inflatable Santa Heist.

Q: What unusual 2013 theft involved the heist of 10,000 gallons of vodka from a distillery in Russia?
A: The Vodka Heist.

Incredible and Odd Coincidences

Explore the realm of incredible coincidences with this trivia section, featuring remarkable historical synchronicities and fateful events.

Discover the uncanny alignments and surprising connections between seemingly unrelated occurrences that have shaped history. From simultaneous discoveries to coincidental encounters, delve into the stories behind these extraordinary moments of serendipity.

This section celebrates the fascinating and often mind-boggling intersections of fate and chance that have left a lasting impact on the world.

Q: Which U.S. President, who was born in 1809, died on the same day as Abraham Lincoln, also born in 1809?
A: William Henry Harrison.

Q: What famous novelist survived the sinking of the RMS Titanic but later died in the sinking of the RMS Lusitania?
A: J. Bruce Ismay (though he wasn't a novelist, he was a notable figure involved in both events).

Q: Which famous author and inventor died exactly 7 years before the sinking of the Titanic, despite predicting its disaster?
A: Mark Twain (who did not predict the Titanic but had a coincidental timing with his death).

Q: What coincidence occurred between the U.S. Presidents William McKinley and Franklin D. Roosevelt, both of whom were shot while in office?
A: Both were shot by assassins, McKinley in 1901 and Roosevelt in 1933, but survived or were not fatally harmed.

Q: What was the coincidence involving the two presidential candidates William Henry Harrison and Martin Van Buren regarding their birthdays?
A: Harrison and Van Buren were both born in 1773 and their presidential campaigns against each other were closely timed.

Q: What was unusual about the deaths of both the Titanic's captain, Edward Smith, and the Lusitania's captain, William Thomas Turner?
A: Both captains were involved in major maritime disasters and died in the tragedies they were part of.

Q: Which 19th-century author and critic had his works published posthumously and was discovered to have predicted many major world events?
A: Jules Verne (he wrote about many inventions and events before they happened).

Q: What is the strange coincidence involving the birth dates of the U.S. Presidents Thomas Jefferson and John Adams?
A: Both Jefferson and Adams died on July 4th, 1826, the 50th anniversary of the Declaration of Independence.

Q: What was notable about the death of the French writer and philosopher Voltaire compared to his contemporary Jean-Jacques Rousseau?
A: Voltaire died on the same day Rousseau was born, which is an example of coincidental timing in intellectual history.

Q: What is the remarkable coincidence involving the American presidents Abraham Lincoln and John F. Kennedy regarding their assassinations?
A: Both presidents were assassinated on a Friday and had a successor named Johnson, who was a Southern Democrat.

Q: What unusual coincidence happened with the death of 19th-century explorer Richard Francis Burton and writer Sir Richard Francis Burton?
A: They shared a name and were both explorers, though they lived in different times.

Q: What historical figure, known for their work in physics, shared a birthday with the famous poet William Wordsworth?
A: Albert Einstein and William Wordsworth both had February 22nd as their birthday.

Q: What was strange about the similarity in the lives of twins separated at birth, Jim Lewis and Jim Springer, who later reunited?
A: They had remarkably similar lives, including identical tastes, careers, and even names for their pets.

Q: What odd coincidence happened to two sets of twins, the Wyrick and the Kuhl twins, who were separated at birth and later met?
A: Both pairs had remarkably similar life experiences, including similar careers and family structures.

Q: Which two famous figures in World War II had a remarkable coincidence involving their names and ranks?
A: Winston Churchill and Charles de Gaulle, both prominent WWII leaders with coincidental historical timings.

Q: What unusual coincidence occurred with the famous composers Ludwig van Beethoven and Wolfgang Amadeus Mozart regarding their deaths?
A: Both died at relatively young ages and were prolific composers whose works became legendary.

Q: What remarkable coincidence occurred with the Titanic's iceberg and the ship's forecast of its arrival?
A: The iceberg that sank the Titanic was sighted by another ship, the Californian, which had failed to warn the Titanic in time.

Q: What is the coincidence involving the world's first and last lunar missions and their timing?
A: The Apollo 11 landing in 1969 was followed by the Apollo 17 mission, which was the final manned lunar landing before the program ended.

Q: What strange similarity existed between the lives of the American inventors Thomas Edison and Nikola Tesla?
A: Both were pioneers in electrical engineering, had public disputes, and died on January 7th, though not the same year.

Q: What is the coincidence involving the 1920s U.S. presidential election and the future of American politics?
A: The 1920 election marked the rise of the Republican Party, which dominated U.S. politics for several decades.

Q: What odd historical coincidence occurred with the assassinations of Archduke Franz Ferdinand and President William McKinley?
A: Both were assassinated in events that led to major global conflicts: World War I and the Spanish-American War.

Q: What peculiar coincidence occurred between the lives of the famous explorers Marco Polo and Christopher Columbus?
A: Both explorers' voyages greatly impacted European understanding of the world and led to significant global events.

Q: What was unusual about the lives of the famous kings Richard the Lionheart and Richard III?
A: Both Richards had remarkable military careers and were pivotal in English history but had very different fates.

Q: What odd coincidence involved the first and last recorded human infections of a specific disease?
A: The first and last documented cases of smallpox in humans occurred in the 20th century before its eradication.

Q: What is the historical coincidence involving the famous 18th-century scientist Benjamin Franklin and the French Revolution?
A: Franklin's diplomatic work in France was influential just as the French Revolution began, leading to significant historical changes.

Q: What strange occurrence involved the end of the Cold War and the fall of the Berlin Wall in 1989?
A: The fall of the Berlin Wall marked a dramatic end to Cold War tensions, coinciding with significant political changes across Europe.

Q: What remarkable coincidence occurred with the famous British Prime Ministers Winston Churchill and Neville Chamberlain?
A: Both were key figures in British politics during World War II, with Churchill succeeding Chamberlain as Prime Minister.

Q: What peculiar historical coincidence involved the assassination of President William Henry Harrison and his successor, John Tyler?

A: Harrison died just 31 days into his presidency, making Tyler the first vice president to assume the office, and Tyler had a unique role in presidential succession.

Q: What was unusual about the coincidence between the death of Martin Luther King Jr. and the assassination of Robert F. Kennedy?
A: Both were prominent civil rights figures assassinated in the 1960s, impacting the course of American history significantly.

Q: What odd coincidence occurred between the lives of the famous scientists Isaac Newton and Albert Einstein?
A: Both made groundbreaking contributions to physics, with their discoveries marking significant advancements in our understanding of the universe.

Q: What peculiar fact links the lives of the famous physicists Richard Feynman and Niels Bohr?
A: Both made influential contributions to quantum mechanics, despite working in different times and locations.

Q: What was unusual about the lives of the famous European explorers Vasco da Gama and Ferdinand Magellan?
A: Both explorers played crucial roles in discovering new maritime routes, leading to major shifts in global trade and exploration.

Q: What odd coincidence happened with the founding dates of the United Nations and the League of Nations?
A: The United Nations was founded after the League of Nations failed to prevent World War II, marking a significant change in international diplomacy.

Q: What strange similarity exists between the lives of the famous Russian leaders Tsar Nicholas II and Joseph Stalin?
A: Both had significant impacts on Russian history, with Nicholas II being the last tsar and Stalin leading the Soviet Union during its most turbulent times.

Q: What is the curious connection between the famous French artists Claude Monet and Edgar Degas?
A: Both were leading figures in the Impressionist movement, despite having differing styles and artistic philosophies.

Q: What notable coincidence occurred with the life of the famous inventor Alexander Graham Bell and the telephone's development?
A: Bell was awarded the first patent for the telephone just before another inventor, Elisha Gray, filed a similar patent.

Q: What unusual historical coincidence involves the famous revolutionary figures Che Guevara and Fidel Castro?
A: Guevara and Castro were both central to the Cuban Revolution and had intertwined careers in the fight against colonial rule.

Q: What peculiar fact connects the famous American presidents George Washington and Abraham Lincoln?
A: Both were instrumental in defining the U.S. government and had significant anniversaries and events marking their contributions.

Q: What was unusual about the historical connection between the French Revolutionary leaders Robespierre and Napoleon Bonaparte?
A: Robespierre's rise and fall paved the way for Napoleon's rise to power during the French Revolution.

Q: What curious coincidence involves the famous British monarchs Henry VIII and Elizabeth I?
A: Both had significant impacts on English history, with Henry's rule leading to the establishment of the Church of England and Elizabeth's reign marking a golden age.

Q: What strange historical event involved the famous American inventor Thomas Edison and his rival Nikola Tesla?
A: Edison and Tesla's "War of Currents" over electrical systems dramatically influenced modern electrical infrastructure.

Q: What odd coincidence occurred with the lives of the famous ancient Greek philosophers Socrates and Plato?
A: Plato was a student of Socrates, whose teachings deeply influenced Plato's philosophical works.

Q: What remarkable coincidence involves the famous military leaders Genghis Khan and Napoleon Bonaparte?
A: Both leaders had extensive military campaigns and significantly shaped the history of their respective regions through their conquests.

Q: What unusual historical event connects the famous explorers Christopher Columbus and Ferdinand Magellan?
A: Both were pivotal in the Age of Exploration, with Columbus discovering the Americas and Magellan circumnavigating the globe.

Q: What peculiar similarity exists between the lives of the famous historical figures Julius Caesar and Augustus?
A: Augustus succeeded Julius Caesar, marking the transition from the Roman Republic to the Roman Empire.

Q: What odd coincidence happened with the famous composers Ludwig van Beethoven and Wolfgang Amadeus Mozart regarding their health?
A: Both experienced significant hearing loss during their lives, yet continued to compose influential music.

Q: What strange historical event involved the famous leaders Winston Churchill and Franklin D. Roosevelt?
A: Churchill and Roosevelt had a close working relationship during World War II, coordinating strategies for the Allied forces.

Q: What peculiar fact connects the famous Russian writers Leo Tolstoy and Fyodor Dostoevsky?
A: Both wrote some of the most influential novels in Russian literature, despite their different styles and themes.

Q: What odd coincidence involves the famous leaders Abraham Lincoln and Jefferson Davis?
A: Both were born in Kentucky and became pivotal figures in the American Civil War, Lincoln as the Union President and Davis as the Confederate President.

Q: What unusual historical event links the famous explorers Marco Polo and Vasco da Gama?
A: Both explorers made significant discoveries that changed European understanding of Asia and the wider world.

Q: What peculiar similarity connects the lives of the famous scientists Charles Darwin and Alfred Russel Wallace?
A: Both independently developed the theory of natural selection, leading to a joint publication on evolution.

Q: What curious coincidence occurred with the lives of the famous American authors Edgar Allan Poe and Nathaniel Hawthorne?
A: Both were influential in American literature, with Poe known for his macabre stories and Hawthorne for his dark romanticism.

Q: What odd fact connects the famous French leaders Napoleon Bonaparte and Charles de Gaulle?
A: Both were influential in French history and had significant impacts on France's military and political landscape.

Q: What unusual historical coincidence involves the famous British Prime Ministers Benjamin Disraeli and William Gladstone?
A: Disraeli and Gladstone were political rivals who served as Prime Ministers during the same period of British history.

Q: What peculiar connection exists between the famous ancient Egyptian rulers Tutankhamun and Ramses II?
A: Both are well-known due to their significant contributions to ancient Egyptian history and their tombs.

Q: What strange coincidence involves the famous British explorer James Cook and the famous American explorer Meriwether Lewis?
A: Both made significant explorations that expanded European knowledge of the Pacific and North America.

Q: What remarkable historical event links the famous artists Leonardo da Vinci and Michelangelo?
A: Both were leading figures in the Italian Renaissance and had a significant impact on Western art and culture.

Q: What peculiar fact connects the famous historical figures William Shakespeare and Miguel de Cervantes?

A: Shakespeare and Cervantes died on the same day, April 23, 1616, though they lived in different countries.

Q: What odd coincidence involves the famous military leaders Alexander the Great and Julius Caesar?
A: Both leaders achieved significant military conquests and had a lasting impact on their respective empires.

Q: What unusual historical event links the famous philosophers Socrates and Confucius?
A: Both Socrates and Confucius were influential in their respective cultures and had profound impacts on Western and Eastern philosophies.

Fantastic Myths and Fables

Discover fantastic fables with this trivia section, showcasing unbelievable yet true stories from history.

Explore incredible accounts that seem too extraordinary to be real, including legendary events and remarkable figures whose tales defy belief. Delve into the facts behind these seemingly fantastical narratives and uncover the truth behind history's most astonishing stories.

This section offers a captivating look at the remarkable and often surprising events that have shaped our past.

Q: What historical figure is believed to have inspired the legend of Robin Hood with his exploits of stealing from the rich and giving to the poor?
A: The real-life outlaw, Robert Hood.

Q: Which ancient Greek mythological figure is known for completing 12 labors, including slaying the Nemean Lion?
A: Heracles (or Hercules).

Q: What was the real name of the notorious pirate who became the legendary figure Blackbeard?
A: Edward Teach.

Q: What is the historical basis for the myth of the fountain of youth that explorers like Ponce de León sought?
A: The legend may have originated from native tales about a life-giving spring, rather than an actual fountain.

Q: Which English monarch was rumored to have been buried with a secret message revealing hidden treasures?
A: Richard III.

Q: What legendary lost city, sought by explorers like Francisco de Orellana, is said to have been located in the Amazon jungle?
A: El Dorado.

Q: Which historical figure was believed to have been able to turn anything he touched into gold, a tale known as the Midas touch?
A: King Midas of Phrygia.

Q: What historical event has given rise to the legend of the "curse of the pharaohs," involving mysterious deaths of those who disturbed Tutankhamun's tomb?
A: The discovery of Tutankhamun's tomb in 1922.

Q: Which Russian tsar was rumored to have a secret society of alchemists attempting to find the elixir of life?
A: Tsar Peter the Great.

Q: Which famous pirate legend involves a hidden treasure buried on a remote Caribbean island, famously detailed by Robert Louis Stevenson?
A: The legend of Treasure Island.

Q: What historical figure's actions are linked to the myth of the "lost" American colony of Roanoke?
A: Sir Walter Raleigh.

Q: What ancient Greek myth involves a hero whose heel was his only vulnerable spot, leading to the term "Achilles' heel"?

A: Achilles.

Q: Which Roman Emperor is associated with the legend of the "Mad Emperor" who allegedly fiddled while Rome burned?
A: Emperor Nero.

Q: What legendary figure, known for his ability to manipulate the weather, was a part of ancient Norse mythology and was connected with thunder?
A: Thor.

Q: Which historical figure is linked to the myth of the "Man in the Iron Mask," a mysterious prisoner in France?
A: The identity of the prisoner remains debated, but he was known as the Man in the Iron Mask.

Q: What famous British legend involves a giant from Cornwall who is said to have built several landmarks by throwing rocks?
A: The legend of Giant's Causeway.

Q: Which historical conspiracy theory alleges that a secret society known as the Illuminati controls world affairs from behind the scenes?
A: The Illuminati Conspiracy.

Q: Which ancient civilization's myths include a serpent-like creature known as Quetzalcoatl, the feathered serpent god?
A: The Aztec civilization.

Q: What medieval legend involves a figure who is said to have protected the realm of Britain and is associated with the sword Excalibur?
A: King Arthur.

Q: What is the name of the legendary warrior princess of China who is said to have disguised herself as a man to fight in place of her elderly father?
A: Hua Mulan.

Q: Which historical figure was involved in the conspiracy theory of the "Dulce Base," alleged to be a secret underground facility for extraterrestrial research?
A: The conspiracy involves various theorists, not a specific historical figure.

Q: Which explorer is associated with the legend of finding a mythical city of gold in the Americas, known as El Dorado?
A: Francisco de Orellana.

Q: What mythological creature from ancient Greek legends is known for its ability to turn people into stone with its gaze?
A: Medusa.

Q: Which British naval officer was believed to have been involved in a conspiracy to uncover hidden treasures in the Caribbean?
A: Sir Francis Drake.

Q: What famous ancient Greek tale involves a labyrinth built by Daedalus to contain a monstrous creature known as the Minotaur?
A: The story of the Minotaur and the Labyrinth.

Q: What mythical creature from Japanese folklore is known for its shape-shifting abilities and is often depicted as a fox?
A: The Kitsune.

Q: What medieval legend involves a magical stone that grants eternal youth and has been sought by various historical figures?
A: The Philosopher's Stone.

Q: Which conspiracy theory alleges that a secret elite group controls global finance and politics and is often associated with shadowy organizations?
A: The New World Order theory.

Q: What is the name of the mythical giant serpent from Scandinavian folklore, said to encircle the world and cause earthquakes when it moves?
A: Jörmungandr (the Midgard Serpent).

Q: What historical figure is associated with the legend of the "Grail King," who was believed to have guarded the Holy Grail?
A: The Fisher King from Arthurian legend.

Q: What legendary creature from Irish folklore is said to live in a hidden underwater kingdom and is known for its magical powers?
A: The Selkie.

Q: Which famous Roman general was rumored to have been buried with treasures in an undisclosed location, leading to myths about his final resting place?
A: Julius Caesar.

Q: What historical conspiracy theory involves a supposed secret plot by the Catholic Church to suppress ancient knowledge and texts?
A: The suppression of the Cathar heresy and Gnostic texts.

Q: What historical figure was rumored to have a hidden underground city filled with treasures, associated with the conspiracy theories about hidden knowledge?
A: The legend of the secret underground city, often tied to figures like Nikola Tesla.

Q: What ancient Egyptian deity was believed to protect the dead and guide them to the afterlife, often depicted with a jackal head?
A: Anubis.

Q: What historical figure is associated with the legend of being buried with an enormous treasure in a hidden location, fueling various treasure hunts?
A: The legend often connects with figures like the Spanish conquistadors and their hidden riches.

Q: Which mythological hero from ancient Greece was famous for his role in the Trojan War and the epic journey home described in the "Odyssey"?
A: Odysseus.

Q: What ancient legend describes a hidden city beneath the Andes, rumored to be filled with gold and precious stones, and is linked to the Inca Empire?
A: The legend of Paititi.

Q: What mythical sea creature from Norse mythology is said to dwell in the oceans and cause storms and shipwrecks?
A: The Kraken.

Q: What ancient Roman legend involves a mysterious being known as the Lares, who were thought to protect household and family?

A: The Lares, or household deities of ancient Rome.

Q: What conspiracy theory involves claims that ancient aliens or extraterrestrial beings influenced human history and technology?
A: Ancient Astronaut Theory.

Q: What famous historical figure was rumored to have discovered a mythical land of immortality, fueling various legends about his travels?
A: The myths often link with figures like the legendary Greek hero, Jason.

Q: What historical figure is associated with the fabled "Lost Continent of Atlantis," often speculated to be a real place in various conspiracy theories?
A: Plato, who first mentioned Atlantis in his writings.

Q: What mythical beast from ancient Chinese legends is said to have the body of a deer, the tail of an ox, and the hooves of a horse?
A: The Qilin.

Q: Which historical event is tied to the legend of the "curse of the mummy," involving the supposed supernatural consequences of disturbing ancient Egyptian tombs?
A: The opening of Tutankhamun's tomb in 1922.

Q: What famous legendary artifact is said to possess miraculous powers and has been the subject of numerous myths and quests throughout history?
A: The Holy Grail.

Q: What historical figure was linked to the myth of having hidden a vast fortune in gold, which remains undiscovered to this day?
A: The myth is often tied to figures like Francisco Pizarro.

Q: What mythical creature from Greek mythology is said to have wings, a lion's body, and a serpent's tail?
A: The Chimera.

Q: What peculiar historical conspiracy involves claims that a secretive group of scientists were working on creating a "time machine" during World War II?
A: The Philadelphia Experiment conspiracy theory.

Q: What ancient Persian mythological figure is associated with the legend of the "Magic Carpet," said to be able to transport people instantly?
A: The legend of the Magic Carpet is rooted in Persian folklore.

Q: What unusual legend involves a mythical "city of mirrors" that was believed to be a hidden paradise with magical properties?
A: The legend of the "City of Mirrors" often associated with Central Asian myths.

Q: What historical figure is linked to the myth of the "Philosopher's Stone," a legendary alchemical substance that could turn base metals into gold?
A: The Philosopher's Stone is tied to historical alchemists like Nicolas Flamel.

Q: What historical conspiracy theory involves the idea that secret societies like the Freemasons control global events from behind the scenes?
A: The Freemason Conspiracy Theory.

Q: What ancient Greek legend involves a hero who travels to the underworld to retrieve his beloved, encountering various mythical creatures?
A: The myth of Orpheus and Eurydice.

Q: What famous mythical creature from Japanese folklore is said to be an immortal being that can turn into a beautiful woman?
A: The Kitsune.

Q: What historical event led to the legend of a cursed treasure associated with a famous British explorer's final expedition?
A: The legend of the curse of Captain James Cook's voyages.

Q: What ancient myth involves a hero who sailed on the Argonauts' ship to retrieve the Golden Fleece, with various supernatural encounters along the way?
A: The myth of Jason and the Argonauts.

Q: What historical figure is linked to the myth of the "Dancing Plague," where people danced uncontrollably and some reportedly died from exhaustion?
A: The Dancing Plague of 1518, associated with Strasbourg, though specific figures are less clear.

Q: What famous mythological figure from Scandinavian folklore is known for his role in Ragnarok, the end of the world battle?
A: Loki.

Q: What peculiar legend involves a hidden "city of gold" that explorers believed existed in North America and is linked to the Spanish conquistadors?
A: The legend of Cibola.

Q: What historical figure was rumored to have hidden a vast amount of wealth in a secret location, leading to ongoing treasure hunts?
A: The treasure legend often ties to figures like Captain Kidd.

Q: What historical myth involves a supposed device that can make people invisible, associated with the famed alchemist Hermes Trismegistus?
A: The myth of the "Cloak of Invisibility" from various ancient texts.

Q: What ancient Greek figure was believed to have constructed a massive labyrinth to imprison the Minotaur?
A: Daedalus.

Q: What legendary creature from Celtic folklore is said to be a magical creature that could grant wishes but only to those who were pure of heart?
A: The Leprechaun.

Q: What historical event is tied to the legend of a supposed "lost" library that contained all the secrets of ancient knowledge?
A: The legendary Library of Alexandria.

Q: What historical figure is associated with a myth involving a magical island that would rise from the ocean once every century?
A: The myth is often connected with figures like Atlantis and Plato.

Q: What historical conspiracy theory involves the belief that ancient knowledge was suppressed to keep certain truths hidden from the public?
A: The Lost Knowledge Theory.

Q: What ancient Greek mythological figure is known for his journey to the underworld and his efforts to bring back his wife?

A: Orpheus.

Q: What famous legend involves a magical horn that could summon powerful storms and was sought after by various explorers?
A: The legend of the "Horn of Roland."

Q: What historical myth involves a supposed race of giants that once inhabited the Earth, according to ancient legends?
A: The myth of the Titans.

Q: What famous conspiracy theory involves the belief that historical figures like Julius Caesar were involved in secret societies controlling history?
A: The Theory of Secret Societies.

Q: What ancient myth involves a king who could turn everything he touched into gold, resulting in his downfall?
A: King Midas.

Q: What peculiar legend involves a mythical beast said to guard a hidden treasure buried in a remote location?
A: The legend of the "Guardian Dragon."

Q: What historical figure is linked to the legend of a mysterious "black book" containing secrets of the supernatural and forbidden knowledge?
A: The legend is often associated with figures like the "Devil's Bible," Codex Gigas.

Q: What famous historical fable involves a supposed island where inhabitants lived in perfect harmony, disconnected from the rest of the world?
A: The fable of Atlantis, as described by Plato.

www.ingramcontent.com/pod-product-compliance
Lightning Source LLC
Chambersburg PA
CBHW051557250726
48653CB00004BA/1199